JEEP CHEROKEE

PERFORMANCE UPGRADES 1984–2001

Eric Zappe

CarTech®

CarTech®

CarTech®, Inc.
39966 Grand Avenue
North Branch, MN 55056
Phone: 651-277-1200 or 800-551-4754
Fax: 651-277-1203
www.cartechbooks.com

Edit by Travis Thompson and Paul Johnson
Layout by Christopher Fayers

ISBN 978-1-61325-176-8
Item No. SA109

Library of Congress Cataloging-in-Publication Data Available

Written, edited, and designed in the U.S.A.
Printed in China
10 9 8 7 6 5 4 3 2 1

Cover: *This Jeep Cherokee XJ navigates and scales the rocks quite well. Although the stock unibody chassis and suspension are adequate for over-the-road use, you need to strengthen the chassis and upgrade suspension components for off-road duty. (Photo Courtesy Eric Zappe)*

Title page: *Mike, Nick, Dustin, Jesse, Tom, and Eric at the Moon-Rocks. Whether you have a stock or lifted Cherokee, a group trail ride can be a very enjoyable outdoor activity.*

Back Cover:

Top Left: *In rock-infested terrain, you can't drive around all the big rocks on the trail. And you certainly don't want to straddle them, because they will damage the underside of your Jeep. The correct technique is to choose a line where the tires climb over the bigger rocks. This keeps the driveline out of harm's way.*

Top Right: *Merge crossovers are precision cut for flow, then carefully TIG welded to seal all seams. This results in a smooth flow transition with minimal exhaust-flow turbulence, in contrast to a straight-balance pipe that's welded at 90 degrees to the main pipes.*

Middle Left: *TeraFlex makes a high-steer knuckle that replaces the stock outer knuckle on the passenger side of the Dana 30. This gives the option of over-the-knuckle steering, but even if the drag link is mounted from below, it is still higher than stock.*

Middle Right: *This is a high-pinion Dana 30. Its pinion is above the centerline of the axle. High-pinion axles are preferred because they offer more driveshaft clearance, better driveshaft angles, and are slightly stronger.*

Bottom Left: *The transfer case sends power to the front driveshaft when 4WD is engaged. It is a critical link to any 4WD system.*

Bottom Right: *The front of Jason's rig sports a Custom 4x4 Fabrication bumper, Warn winch with synthetic winch rope, and Light Force 170 off-road lights. (Photo courtesy Jason West)*

OVERSEAS DISTRIBUTION BY:

PGUK
63 Hatton Garden
London EC1N 8LE, England
Phone: 020 7061 1980 • Fax: 020 7242 3725
www.pguk.co.uk

Renniks Publications Ltd.
3/37-39 Green Street
Banksmeadow, NSW 2109, Australia
Phone: 2 9695 7055 • Fax: 2 9695 7355
www.renniks.com

CONTENTS

Eric Zappe has been around Jeeps for many years. In late 1999, he bought his first XJ, a brand-new 2000 Cherokee Sport from the factory. He still owns that Jeep; it is now transformed into a highly modified rock-crawler named *Project Rubicon*. The early stages of this build are featured in this book. Eric also has a 1997 Sport Cherokee, which serves as a daily driver. This Cherokee has a 2-inch budget boost and 30-inch tires.

Reno, Nevada, is home for Eric, his wife, and two children. He has always been drawn to the outdoors and enjoys hiking and exploring new areas. The Jeep Cherokee was an ideal vehicle that could help get to remote camping spots in the Sierra Nevada Mountains, which are close to home.

The Cherokee began as a hobby that has gone way out of control. Eric is a member of several online forums including NAXJA (North American XJ Association); he is currently president of the Sierra Chapter. Eric's Jeep has been featured in *JP Magazine* (January 2014) in addition to several online forums and Jeep-related websites including his own: ericsxj.com. Eric also believes in protecting our access to public lands and is a member of the Blue Ribbon Coalition and the Nevada Four Wheel Drive Association.

Acknowledgments

I would like to thank the following people for help with this book. Whether they realize it or not, I depended very much on their support, and the book would not have been possible if I had tried to do it alone. Jim Jackson of ARB USA; Jason of Red Rock 4x4; Matt of T&T Customs; Greg of C-ROK; Perry at Reno Driveline Service; Jason West; Garrett Bird; Jesse Reeves; Lee Harper; Mark Tener; Jacob Fisher; Bryan Vetrano; John Laurella; Phil Weeks; Pete Montie; Tom, Dustin, Travis, Mike, Matt, David and the rest of the Reno 4x4 crew; JeepForum.com; NAXJA; my editors Travis Thompson and Paul Johnson; and everyone else behind the scenes at CarTech Books. A special thanks goes to my family for their love and support.

Author Eric Zappe with his son Taylor and Project Rubicon, *Eric's 2000 Patriot Blue Jeep Cherokee.*

Eric owns two Jeep Cherokees: Project Rubicon, *a 2000 XJ (left) with roughly 6 inches of lift and 35s, and a 1997 XJ (right) that is mostly stock.*

This book was written to show how an average Jeep Cherokee can be modified into a highly capable 4x4 trail machine. It will guide you through each of the major systems, from the suspension to the axles and driveline, discussing the most common and basic upgrades and moving on to more advanced modifications. You may already know what type of build-up you would like to do, or you may not have gotten that far yet. Either way, I'm sure this book will give you some ideas and inspire you to reach your goals.

Daily Driver, Trail Rig, or Both?

There are several things you should consider for your build-up: Will your Jeep be a daily driver or a dedicated trail rig? Will it be modified for mainly street use and good looks, or will it be built to handle punishing terrain and look bad-ass at the same time? What type of terrain will you run? Mud? Rocks? A little bit of everything? How about a Jeep built for lengthy expeditions into remote areas that can handle all types of terrain with confidence?

This 1988 XJ gets beaten hard, and the owner, Christopher Corpus, enjoys every bit of it. That's what it was built for: having fun off-road. I'm not sure if the right word to describe it is "built," because it looks like more stuff was taken off than added to it!

This 1997 two-door is a good example of an XJ that is built to handle some very tough trails. Mike Hobbs has kept it very drivable for the street, too. It has 4.10:1 gears, 33-inch tires, and a manual transmission. For off-road, he has a TeraFlex 4:1 low-range transfer case and a nice Rubicon Express suspension.

Even two-wheel-drive (2WD) XJs can be built to compete on the JeepSpeed racing circuit. The Jeep Cherokee is a

Steve Doty pushes his Jeep to the limits, and sometimes things don't turn out as planned! With the right modifications, you can afford to take a few risks now and then, but knowledge and experience will teach you what risks to take and which ones to avoid.

great platform to start from, but where it ends up is completely up to you!

This book will also show you what compromises you'll make when you modify your Cherokee. This will be most important if you plan on keeping your Cherokee a daily driver yet at the same time making it capable enough to handle extreme terrain. When you modify something, a compromise is made. How big or small that compromise will be is relative to your goals. If you're building a rig that will be trailered to and from the trails, you might not care about having air conditioning, interior carpet, or even doors. On the other hand, you might care a lot about the drop in fuel efficiency when you slap on those huge tires. One thing to keep in mind is that when you modify your Jeep you should be modifying it for the better. The compromises you make will be worth it if you plan ahead and know where you want to end up.

Project Rubicon

Among the many different Cherokee build-ups that are featured in this book, I also talk about my own Cherokee, which I have named *Project Rubicon*. It started out as a Patriot Blue 2000 Jeep Cherokee Sport that I bought new in 1999. Soon after I bought it, I began modifying it for off-road use. It was a great vehicle for camping and scenic backcountry trail rides, but I knew I wanted it to be capable of much more. Living about an hour from Lake Tahoe and the world-famous Rubicon Trail, I knew that one day I wanted to complete that trail. But this was also my daily driver and our family's primary vehicle, so I had to take into consideration its on-road comfort as well as off-road capability. After all, I still had several years of payments to make on this thing, so I couldn't just make it a dedicated trail rig . . . yet.

Many people who enjoy the outdoors use their Cherokees to take them to amazing places that they might not otherwise see. Building your Jeep the right way not only ensures a safe trip, but can make getting there just as fun! (Photo Courtesy John Laurella)

Jeep XJ Profile: *Project Rubicon*

Rubicon (roo'bi-kon') n. A limit that when passed allows no return. (*Webster's II New College Dictionary*).

Year: 2000
Engine: 4.0L I-6
Transmission: AW4 automatic
Transfer Case: NP231 + "hack-n-tap" SYE
Front Axle: High-pinion Dana 30
Rear Axle: Chrysler 8.25
Gears: 4.56:1
Lockers: Front and rear ARB Air Lockers
Steering: Currie HD
Suspension: RE 5.5-inch Extreme Duty Short-Arm
Shocks: RE Monotubes
Tires: 35 x 12.50-inch TrXus MT
Wheels: 15 x 8–inch steel Rockcrawlers

Project Rubicon *started out as a new 2000 Cherokee Sport. Since then, it has gradually evolved into a highly capable four-wheeler.*

Project Rubicon *was built with the Rubicon Trail in mind, but it finds itself at home in a variety of terrain found in Nevada and California.*

Project Rubicon was built to handle the tough, tight, rocky trails of the Sierra Nevadas, including the world-famous Rubicon Trail. It has been a work in progress ever since the first "modifications" (a locking gas cap and ski racks), and it is now a very capable off-road XJ.

The suspension has gone through a couple of stages of upgrades along the way. The first lift was the Rubicon Express 4.5-inch kit. I ran 31-inch Goodyear MT/Rs, which are admittedly a little small for that much lift. But that was okay at the time, because I was undecided as to how I wanted to trim the fenders and I didn't want too much power loss running big tires with stock 3.55:1 gears. I also opted to use the 4.5-inch leaf packs instead of the 3.5-inch leaf packs and extended shackle. Initially, the 4.5-inch leaf packs gave me 6.5 inches of lift with the Jeep unloaded. They settled down to a little over 5 inches after a few months, but I still ended up adding 3/4-inch Daystar coil spacers to the front to level it. This suspension worked well for two years, but by then I couldn't wait to go bigger.

Next, I upgraded the suspension to the RE 5.5-inch kit with control-arm drop brackets. This allowed me to keep the 4.5-inch leaf springs, which were well broken in by then. This time the front coils netted 6.5 inches, so I swapped the RE shackles for taller TeraFlex shackles to bring the rear of the Jeep up to 6.5 inches. The lower control arms are fixed length, but I upgraded to adjustable uppers to get the Super-Flex joints. The front and rear bumpstops have been extended and bar-pin eliminators have been added to the Rubicon Express monotube shocks for more length to maximize the amount of flex. I trimmed the fenders and raised

Jeep XJ Profile: *Project Rubicon* CONTINUED

This custom onboard air system uses a Viair 400C compressor. It is used for running air lockers and filling tires.

Project Rubicon *was one of the few Jeeps lucky enough to get the AEV rear bumper and tire carrier before the company stopped making them. It holds a 35-inch full-size spare with no problem.*

Strong aftermarket bumpers, rock rails, differential guards, and other skid plates keep it well protected in the rocks.

the stock flares to make room for 33 x 12.50–inch MT/Rs. After running the 33s for a year, I gave the fenders another round of trimming and ditched the stock flares. This made room for the Interco 35 x 12.50–inch TrXus MTs.

The front low-pinion Dana 30 has been replaced by a high-pinion Dana 30 out of a 1998 XJ. It's stuffed with 4.56:1 gears and an ARB Air Locker. It also has the Warn 5-on-4.5 hub conversion, along with Warn alloy inner shafts. The rear axle is the stock 29-spline 8.25-inch Chrysler, upgraded with Yukon 4.56:1 gears and shafts, an ARB locker, and TeraFlex disc brakes. I added 1-inch wheel spacers in the rear to match the wider track of the front axle with the hub kit. I like how much the tires stick out with the 1-inch spacers and 4.5 inches of backspacing on the wheels.

This XJ is well armored for the rocks with front and rear differential guards, control-arm skids, a Rusty's transfer case skid, Tomken gas tank skid, and Rocky Road Outfitters rock rails with custom reinforcements. The front bumper is BPI Fab bumper with a 2-inch receiver and a C-Rok steering box welded to the bumper mounts. The rear bumper and tire carrier is the elusive American Expedition Vehicles XJ bumper (only a few have been produced to date). Rock lights

illuminate the terrain below, and I've mounted IPF 868s on the front bumper. The steering is the Currie HD system, and I've flipped the tie-rod above the knuckle using the Goferit Offroad tie-rod flip insert.

The 4.0L engine is upgraded with a 60-mm throttle body, oversized Mobil 1 oil filter, and DynoMax exhaust. An ARB snorkel provides cold-air induction as well as deep-water fording capability. LeBaron hood vents help cool the engine bay, while the transmission is cooled by a Hayden No. 405 cooler.

Interior modifications include a floor with Herculiner, Cobra CB, and a Viair 400C air compressor mounted in the passenger rear corner where the cubby hole used to be. This electric compressor is part of a custom onboard air system that I use to operate the ARB lockers and fill tires. It includes a 2.5-gallon air tank (mounted under the Jeep), an in-dash illuminated pressure gauge, and hose connects at both ends of the Jeep.

Other photos and updates to *Project Rubicon* can be seen on ericsxj.com. ∎

CHEROKEE BASICS

American Motors Corporation developed and built the Jeep Cherokee XJ. Entering the automotive market in the 1984 model year, the XJ is often referred to as the "down-sized Cherokee" to distinguish it from its older brothers, the full-size Cherokee and Grand Wagoneers of the 1960s, 1970s, and 1980s.

This new downsized Cherokee was given the designation "XJ," which doesn't really stand for anything. It's just a vehicle code from the manufacturer, like YJ and TJ for the Wranglers and ZJ and WJ for the Grand Cherokees. The Cherokee XJ includes all the downsized Cherokee models, such as the different trim levels: Wagoneer, Pioneer, Chief, Laredo, Limited, Sport, Country, Classic, etc.

The 1984 Cherokee XJ was a big hit and was named "4x4 of the Year" by several automotive magazines, including Petersen's *4-Wheel & Off-Road*. Being roughly 1,000 pounds lighter than the full-size Jeeps and considerably smaller in size, the XJ was more maneuverable on the trail and friendlier on the street with better fuel efficiency. As such, the Cherokee XJ became the first compact four-door SUV. It set

With more than 2.8 million Jeep Cherokees produced between 1984 and 2001, the XJ was one of the most popular SUVs ever made. Even after production ceased in 2001, the XJ's popularity as an off-road vehicle has continued to rise. This is a stock 1992 XJ.

the standard for all the auto manufacturers that attempted to imitate it in the years to come.

The Cherokee's lighter weight is attributed to its unibody construction, where the body and frame are one, as opposed to a body-on-frame design used by the full-sized trucks and Jeep Wranglers. Make no mistake, even though the unibody construction is more car-like, the four-wheel-drive (4WD) Cherokee XJ is a real 4x4

John Lewis purchased his 1996 XJ from the State of California Parks and Recreation Department. Many fleet vehicles were the base-model Cherokee without many of the "frills" that the higher-end models had. Some older base-model XJs even came without carpet!

with solid front and rear axles and a low-range transfer case. The Cherokee soon proved itself as a true Jeep by being able to handle off-road terrain quite well, and being smaller and lighter really helped. With an average cargo capacity of 70 cubic feet, it was not only the perfect SUV, but also a true "utility" vehicle that was great for hauling a lot more than just groceries! This also made the Cherokee an ideal fleet vehicle for agencies including the U.S. Forest Service, U.S. Postal Service, and utility companies. Beginning in 1992, there was even a special Police Package that was used by law enforcement agencies throughout the United States.

The Cherokee was a very popular automobile overseas as well. In fact, Jeep produced right-hand-drive XJs with a turbo-diesel engine primarily for export to countries in Europe and South America. Cherokees were sent to China, Japan, Australia, and New Zealand, among others. It is interesting to note that even though the Cherokee XJ has been discontinued in the United States, it is still being produced in China by Beijing Jeep Corporation in cooperation with DaimlerChrysler. Their Super Cherokee and Jeep 2500 models are based off of the older-body-style XJ, but they are new vehicles with updated styling and features.

In the United States, the production of the Cherokee XJ lasted 18 years, ending with the 2001 model. During this period, 2,884,172 Cherokees were built.

Buying a Cherokee

Whether you're looking for a Cherokee to buy or you already have one, you need to know what you're starting with. There were several

The young owner of this broken 1986 XJ found out the hard way why these 2.8L XJs aren't the best to build. He went through numerous GKN shafts and his 2.8L V-6 was very underpowered, especially for a lifted rig with big tires. Electrical problems were the final straw, and he eventually swapped the lift and axles onto another XJ.

changes to the XJ during its 18-year production run, and some of those changes have a big effect on how the XJ performs off-road, either stock or in the beginning stages of your build-up. If you're looking at doing an extreme build-up, just about any XJ will do, because you will be swapping out a lot of the stock drivetrain. But there are still some important considerations, especially if you're likely to be using some or all of the stock drivetrain to start out with. Below is a listing by year of what to look for; refer to the Appendix (page 138) for a more detailed listing of stock specs.

1984–1986

These Cherokees should be avoided for a few reasons. The big one is the fact that they were only offered with the 2.5L 4-cylinder engine or the GM 2.8L V-6 engine. Most people with the 2.8L V-6 are unsatisfied with the amount of power

Most 1984–1986 XJs have the GKN front driveshaft (left), which is significantly weaker than the Spicer driveshaft (right). The GKN's CV joint doesn't like tall lifts very much, either. It is possible to convert the yoke to run the Spicer driveshaft, but if you can avoid these XJs to begin with, that's just one less thing you have to worry about.

and want to do an engine swap. Because it's a GM engine, swapping in GM's more-powerful 3.4L V-6 is the best option. Unfortunately, there are other problems with these first

XJs. They have an inferior GKN front driveshaft with a CV joint that enthusiasts call the "stick in a can." This CV joint doesn't like operating at steeper angles, so guys with tall lifts wear these joints out very fast. The 1984–1986 transfer cases (NP207, NP228, NP229) also have a slightly higher low-range ratio of 2.61:1, as opposed to the later NP231 and NP242, which have a 2.72:1 ratio. This difference with the low-range ratio is minor, but I thought it was worth a mention. The main issue with these XJs is the lack of a powerful engine, but because these are the oldest XJs, they also likely have more wear and tear, and possibly rust.

The Vacuum-Disconnect Front Axle

Many XJs built between 1984 and 1991 have a vacuum-disconnect Dana 30 front axle. This is easily identifiable by the housing, which wraps around the passenger-side axle tube. Inside the housing, a shift fork engages the front axle when the transfer case lever is pulled into 4WD. Due to wear and tear on these aging

vehicles, this vacuum disconnect system is often problematic, making it difficult to shift in and out of 4WD. Trying to troubleshoot and repair a faulty vacuum-disconnect system can be a major headache. Instead, the vacuum disconnect can be eliminated, and the two-piece axle shaft can then be replaced with a shaft from a non-disconnect axle and new axle seals.

The vacuum-disconnect front axle can be identified by the shift motor housing on the passenger side of the axle. On this axle, the vacuum lines have already been removed in preparation to eliminate the vacuum disconnect.

1987–1989

Some of these XJs came with a strong Dana 44 rear axle, making them the jewels of the junkyards. Due to their age, however, you should probably replace the old axle shafts with new alloy shafts. The old shafts can always be kept as spares. The 4.0L I-6 engine first appeared in 1987 and was a big upgrade from the previous 2.8L V-6. Unfortunately, these XJs (along with the 1990 model

I pulled this Dana 44 out of an XJ at the junkyard. The Dana 44 can be identified by the shape of its cover; it's not oval like the D35, and it doesn't have the flat bottom of the Chrysler 8.25. Instead, it has more of a pointed bottom and looks similar to an apple lying on its side.

This is the front view of the vacuum-disconnect axle. It looks beefy with the extra housing for the shift motor, but I doubt if it is any stronger than the non-disconnect axle.

This is the more reliable non-disconnect axle. You can see that it's a solid tube with no shift motor housing. Some axles prior to 1992 were non-disconnect, but all axles from 1992 and on are non-disconnect.

Changing radiators from the closed pressure-bottle system to one with a radiator cap is fairly easy. You'll need a radiator with a radiator cap, an overflow bottle, a new heater valve, and new hoses.

This 1988 XJ has the closed cooling system. This photo shows the pressure bottle used with this system, secured with a cheesy rubber strap.

and possibly some 1991s) came with a "closed" cooling system that uses a pressure bottle and a radiator without a radiator cap. Many people who have problems with this cooling system find that converting it to the more efficient open-style cooling system is relatively easy and worthwhile. The conversion is very straightforward; just swap in a radiator for a 1992 or newer XJ, a new heater valve (also from 1992 or newer), new hoses, and a new coolant overflow bottle.

The AW4 automatic transmission was first released in 1987, replacing the 3-speed Torqueflite. The AW4 is a 4-speed transmission, with fourth gear being overdrive. The AW4 is a Japanese transmission built by Aisin-Warner that was also used in some Toyotas. The 1987–1991 XJs with the AW4 have a "Power/Comfort" switch on the dash. This switch adjusts the shift points of the transmission. When "Power" is selected, the transmission upshifts at a higher speed and downshifts more quickly. "Comfort" mode upshifts at lower speeds. From 1992 on, this switch was deleted and the shift points are fixed in "Power" mode.

One other difference is that AW4s from 1987 to 1990 have a 21-spline output shaft. In mid-1990, the switch was made to a 23-spline shaft that is not only stronger but more common to mate up with other transfer cases, both stock and aftermarket.

1989–1994

In 1989, ABS (anti-lock brake system) brakes first appeared in the

Cherokees as an option. XJs with ABS received stronger front axle shafts with the larger 5-297x U-joints. The downside is that you get ABS, which many people prefer to do without, especially for off-road use. XJs built in 1992 and later all used the non-disconnect front axle. In 1991 the 4.0L engines were improved with multi-point fuel injection, earning them the "High Output," or "H.O." designation. This new 4.0L H.O. engine put out 190 hp, compared to 177 hp for the non-H.O. engines. In 1991, Chrysler began using the 8.25-inch rear axle in some XJs. This axle has 27-spline shafts and doesn't offer any big benefits over the Dana 35.

1995

All axle shaft assemblies from 1995 and newer have the stronger 5-297x U-joints. A driver-side airbag was also added.

1996

In 1996, Chrysler made a change to the rear driveshaft slip yoke. Before 1996, the slip yoke was encased in an extension housing of the transfer

The transfer cases on pre-1996 XJs have an extension housing that covers the driveshaft's slip yoke. This housing adds support to the slip yoke, which is why these vehicles tend to have less vibration when lifted.

The 1996-and-newer XJs lack the extension housing that came on earlier models. Because there is less support between the bearing of the output shaft and the driveshaft's U-joint, this design is more prone to developing vibrations when the angle of the driveshaft increases, like after a lift kit is installed.

case and was internally lubricated by the transfer case fluid. On the 1996 and newer XJs, there is no extension housing covering the slip yoke. Instead, the splines are pre-greased and covered by a rubber boot to keep them clean. This newer design is more prone to driveline vibrations if you install a lift kit. The common fix for this is a Slip Yoke Eliminator kit (SYE) described on page 91.

1997–1999

For 1997, the XJ was redesigned with a new body style. Most noticeable on the exterior is different plastic trim, fender flares, and bumper end caps. The rear hatch was changed from fiberglass to metal, and the windshield washer bottle was taken out of the engine compartment and relocated inside the driver-side fender. The interior was changed dramatically with a new dash that included a passenger-side airbag. New plastic trim pieces line the interior.

The Dana 35 axle can be identified by the oval cover and oval differential housing. While not visible on this dirty axle, you can also look for "D35" molded into the webbing at the corners where the axle tube is pressed into the housing.

The flat bottom of the Chrysler 8.25-inch rear axle can be recognized from a distance if you know what to look for. The differential cover is oval, but you can still see the flat bottom of the housing below it. The 3-inch axle tubes are also larger than both the Dana 35 and Dana 44.

Along with the cosmetic changes, XJs were upgraded with the Chrysler 8.25-inch axle with 29-spline shafts. All Cherokees with ABS brakes still came with the weaker Dana 35 axle, but XJs without ABS had a good chance of getting the stronger 29-spline 8.25, which is a decent axle, nearly as strong as the Dana 44 with 30-spline shafts.

2000–2001

Two big changes occurred with the last two years of the XJ. Previous to 2000, all XJs came with high-pinion Dana 30 front axles. For the 2000 and 2001 models, they switched to a low-pinion Dana 30 that is identical to that put into the TJ Wranglers. The low pinion isn't as good because it can cause driveline vibrations with taller lifts due to poor pinion angle. Also, the ring-and-pinion isn't quite as strong as the reverse-cut high-pinion gears. In 2000, they also started using the more modern distributorless ignition, which did away with the distributor and spark-plug wires.

These Cherokees also came with the 0331 cylinder heads that have been known to crack between the number-3 and number-4 cylinders on the top. This was due to bad casting at the manufacturer. Although not all 0331 heads crack, it is definitely something to watch for, particularly if the engine has ever overheated. The telltale sign of a cracked head is coolant seeping into the oil. A cracked head isn't the end of the world; it can be replaced with a 2003 or newer head from a TJ or with an aftermarket head. Although there are a ton of differences between the various models, many of the less-desirable parts can be swapped out or upgraded in the course of your build-up. I have always been a believer in the "If it breaks, replace it with something better" philosophy, but I also subscribe to the "Upgrade before it breaks, so it doesn't leave you stranded" theory. If I were looking for another XJ to build, I'd prefer to start with the newest Cherokee I could find, or the one that is in the best condition and as rust-free as possible.

Can My Stock XJ Go Off-Road?

Can your stock XJ go off-road? You bet it can! Cherokees were designed to handle off-road driving in a variety of terrain. You'd be surprised to find out what a stock Cherokee is capable of. In fact, it's a good idea to become familiar with how your Jeep handles in off-road terrain before you start lifting and modifying it. This makes you a better driver and helps you choose your upgrades because you know your Cherokee's capabilities and limitations. That's why this chapter is important. By learning the basics and practicing before you start throwing on a lift and bigger tires, you are much better prepared, understand how everything works, and know how your modifications affect the way your Jeep handles. This chapter was written to get you started: understanding the basics of the Jeep Cherokee and the basics of off-road driving. We must all learn to crawl before we walk or run.

Even though the stock Cherokee is a capable 4x4, the novice wheeler could easily find himself in over his head if the terrain is too difficult for the Jeep and driver's skill. Start out on an easy fire road or gravel road close to home. Practice shifting into low-range and get used to how it feels. As you become comfortable with driving in 4WD, you can try trails that are a little more challenging. The best thing to do is join a local Jeep or 4WD club in your area. Experienced off-roaders can give you valuable advice and would likely be willing to go with you on some easier trails, or let you tag along on more difficult ones. Either way, running with another vehicle is always recommended. That way if you get stuck, at least you won't be stranded or worse.

Jacob Fisher wheels his stock 2001 XJ. Even in stock form, Jeep Cherokees are capable 4x4 vehicles. Getting familiar with how your Jeep handles off-road when stock will help you be a better driver after you start to modify it. Start on easy trails and gradually take on more difficult ones as your driving skills improve.

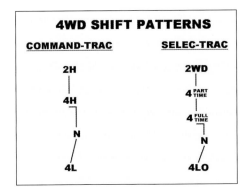

This is the Command-Trac 4WD shift lever with 1997 and newer interior trim. "2H" is two-wheel drive, "4H" is four-wheel drive in high range, and "4L" is four-wheel drive in low range.

Shifting into 4WD

There are two 4WD systems for the Cherokee. The Command-Trac system with the NP231 transfer case is part-time only, and the Selec-Trac system with the NP242 transfer case has both a part-time and full-time 4WD mode. The terms "part-time" and "full-time" can be confusing, so I briefly explain these systems and describe when they should and should not be used.

Part-Time 4WD

Think of "part-time" as meaning "not on pavement." People often mistakenly believe that part-time means that it is sometimes engaged and sometimes it isn't, when in fact it's exactly the opposite. When the 4WD lever is pulled into either the 4H or 4L position, the transfer case delivers power to the front driveshaft (the rear driveshaft is always under power). Both driveshafts turn at the same rate at all times and on all surfaces. However, when turning, the rear wheels follow a different path than the front wheels. Because they're on different paths in the turn, the distance each travels is different. The transfer case does not differentiate, or compensate, for this difference, so wheel slippage is needed. The driveshafts are virtually locked together, so when the front

wheels try to turn at different speeds than the rear wheels, it causes the driveshafts to bind up. If done excessively, damage to the transfer case or driveshafts can occur. For this reason, you should never use part-time 4WD on dry pavement because the tires have too much traction and the wheels are not allowed to slip. Even on wet pavement, you may have too much traction for part-time 4WD. Part-time is okay for snow-covered or icy roads and for all off-road use, including dirt and gravel roads.

Full-Time 4WD

When in full-time mode (Selec-Trac only), the transfer case does differentiate between different driveshaft speeds, so turning on dry pavement is not a problem. You may use full-time 4WD in any condition, wet or dry, all year long.

Selec-Trac systems have a part-time mode and a full-time mode, which are both in high-range. 4LO is part-time low-range. I like to think of full-time mode as on-road 4WD and the part-time modes as off-road 4WD.

Shifting from 2WD to 4H can be done "on the fly," at any safe speed,

without putting the transmission into neutral. Obviously, if the roads are snowy and icy, you should be traveling at a slower than normal speed. If you're going 65 mph you don't need 4WD! Slow down first to a safe speed appropriate for the conditions, and then shift into 4WD. Shifting out of 4H back into 2WD can be done on the fly as well.

When off-road, high-range is used when the trail isn't very difficult (like a fire road) and you wish to travel at a good rate of speed. You should shift into low-range when the trail demands slower vehicle speed but more torque (power) to the wheels. Examples of when low-range should be used are: climbing over large obstacles (rocks, logs, etc.), steep hill climbs, and steep descents. Don't wait until you are halfway through an obstacle to decide you need low-range; shift before you attempt the obstacle. It's also an inconvenience to constantly shift in and out of low-range. If there are other obstacles ahead, just leave it in low-range until it is no longer needed and you want to travel faster. Low-range really isn't that low, and guys with bigger tires who still have stock gears usually end up running low-range through the whole trail.

Shifting into 4L can be tricky sometimes. Reduce your speed to 2 or 3 mph, or you can try it at a complete stop. Shift the transmission to neutral (or depress the clutch pedal if you have a manual transmission). Then shift the 4WD lever through neutral (N) and with a firm tug, into 4L. The owner's manual says to try it at 2 or 3 mph, as this helps the gears line up and mesh properly. I find that with the automatic transmission, it's too difficult to try to shift into

4L when moving, so I always do it from a complete stop. Sometimes it doesn't go right in, but letting off the brake and allowing the Jeep to roll forward or backward slightly usually does the trick. Once in 4L, shift the transmission back into gear and off you go! Shifting out of 4L is done in the same manner; stop, transmission to neutral, shift out of 4L, transmission to drive, and go.

Basic Driving Tips and Techniques

When driving off-road, your number-one concern should be the safety of yourself, your passengers, and your vehicle. The following tips will help you get there and back safely, and being a better driver off-road allows you to have more fun while you're at it. But no matter how much you read, nothing can compare to real-life experience. If you are a beginner, start out with easy trails and gain experience as you progress to more difficult obstacles.

Wear your seatbelt. Even at a crawling speed, a rollover can be sudden and unexpected. Your seatbelt is your number-one defense against being killed or seriously injured in a rollover accident.

Go with at least one other vehicle. If something should break or someone gets injured, you won't be stranded.

Make sure your vehicle is properly equipped and in good working order. At a minimum, you should carry a fire extinguisher, first aid kit, some food and water, and a basic set of tools.

Airing down the tires gives a more comfortable ride on a rough road and can improve your traction. Airing down also increases the size of the tire's footprint. This is very helpful

Rollovers, or "flops," like this are always a possibility. Always wear a seatbelt and keep cargo tied down to reduce the risk of injury. (Photo Courtesy John Laurella)

in sandy terrain, for instance, to help keep your vehicle on top of the sand instead of digging into it. How low you can safely air down depends on the tire and wheel width and the terrain. The lower the air pressure, the larger the footprint, but at the same time there is more risk of unseating the tire's bead from the rim. If you air down, make sure that you have a way to air back up. For stock tires, even those 12-volt plug-in air compressors do the job.

If you aren't driving in the Baja 500 or a Jeepspeed race, don't pretend you are. Slow down. Off-road

In rock-infested terrain, you can't drive around all the big rocks on the trail. And you certainly don't want to straddle them, because they will damage the underside of your Jeep. The correct technique is to choose a line where the tires climb over the bigger rocks. This will keep the driveline out of harm's way.

"Off-camber" is when the sloped terrain causes the vehicle to lean. It can give you an uneasy feeling, like you are about to tip over, which can happen if you aren't careful. In this photo, I don't think Jason is at risk of rolling it, thanks to the trees, but I'm sure he isn't too comfortable! (Photo Courtesy Jason West)

Signs help remind people to use the trails responsibly. Unfortunately, there are always some idiots out there who think the signs are for target practice! We'll see how long this sign lasts. The one above it already has bullet holes.

driving is seldom like in the car commercials where they are flying along at near highway speeds. Bad things often happen when you go too fast.

Climb up and over objects; don't straddle them. For example, if you come across a larger rock in the center of the trail that you cannot go around, crawl slowly over it with your tire rather than trying to let it pass under the center of your Jeep. If you straddle the object and don't have enough clearance, you risk damage to your driveline and/or you have a greater risk of becoming stuck.

Know the depth of water crossings. If unsure, get out and inspect the crossing and look for obstacles that might be under water. If you are still unsure how deep it is or if it is deep with a fast-moving current, it's best not to attempt the crossing. I

violated this rule and got stuck while testing my snorkel and my interior got soaked!

Always go straight up a hill. Never drive up a steep incline at an angle, since the risk of rolling is much higher than if you go straight up. If you don't make it to the top, back straight down. Never try to turn the vehicle around on a steep incline.

For steep descents, put the vehicle in the lowest gear possible and let the engine compression keep the vehicle from going fast. Supplement with the brakes lightly and only as needed. If you use the brakes to slow down, you might accidentally lock them up, which sends you down the hill faster and without steering control.

For extreme off-camber situations, a rollover can often be avoided by turning sharply downhill, or into

the roll. Your instincts might be to turn uphill, but that often causes you to roll over rather than prevent it.

If you can't cross an obstacle in the first one or two attempts, back up and choose a different line of approach. There's no sense beating on your vehicle over and over trying the same thing that isn't working. Use a spotter to guide you through difficult sections as needed.

If you violate the rule about going by yourself and you get stuck, assess the situation and formulate a plan for how to get unstuck. Placing objects like rocks or wood under the tires for traction may work, or you may need to use the jack to raise the vehicle, then place rocks under the wheels. No matter what you do, think and act safely.

After driving off-road, inspect the vehicle completely for any damage.

Responsible Use: Doing Your Part

Across the country, our access to trails is being threatened by activists who would like nothing more than to deny you motorized access to public lands. Many trails have already been closed, and several more are targeted for closure unless we step up to the plate and fight to protect our right to enjoy the outdoors. If we don't do our part to keep public trails open, it won't be long before the only places you are allowed to wheel are at privately owned off-road parks where you have to pay to enter.

One of my favorite things to do is go camping away from as many people as possible, surrounded by the awe-inspiring Sierra Nevada Mountains. Having a 4WD vehicle helps me get to those areas, and in many cases getting there is half the fun. But there have been times when I have pulled up to a trailhead only to find a gate with a "Trail Closed" sign. Even in my local community, I have seen access to public trails become increasingly restricted.

We all must act responsibly when we off-road. It only takes the actions of a few to make us all look really bad, and it's usually those bad actions that stick out for others to see. In order for you to be part of the solution instead of part of the problem, you must:

- Only drive on designated trails and never create your own trail.
- Never create a bypass to an obstacle just because you are unprepared or are afraid of scratching the paint. Maybe that is an indication that you should not be on that trail.
- Never litter. Leave the trail cleaner than you found it by picking up other people's trash.
- Respect others using the trail.
- Always ask permission before entering private property.
- Help by educating others.

In many parts of the country, finding legal places to go wheeling is a challenge. The members of a 4WD club in your area know where the wheeling spots are, or you could probably even get information by asking the guys at a local 4WD shop. Online forums are another way of finding other people in your area who enjoy off-roading. One of the best sources of information is the U.S. Forest Service (fs.fed.us), which has information about recreation on public lands in each state.

One way to become better informed on land-use issues is to become a member of the Blue Ribbon Coalition, United Four Wheel Drive Association, Friends of the Rubicon, or a similar group. These organizations are dedicated to keeping trails open for everyone to enjoy. Let's do our part!

Basic Maintenance and Do-It-Yourself

Vehicles driven off-road generally need more maintenance and upkeep than street-only rides. When you venture far from pavement, you want to have confidence in your vehicle. You want it to perform as it should, but if it isn't well maintained, the chances of something breaking and leaving you stranded increase greatly. For the first time out, here is a brief list of things to check before you go:

- Are the fluids topped off, and are there any leaks that need to be repaired?
- Are your tires in good condition, and do you have a useable spare?
- Can you shift in and out of 4WD; have you really tested it?
- Have the steering linkages and driveshaft grease fittings been lubricated?
- Are the serpentine belt and radiator hoses in good condition?
- Are the axle-shaft U-joints in good condition?
- Are there any known mechanical issues that haven't been fixed yet (overheating, fuel system problems, etc.)?

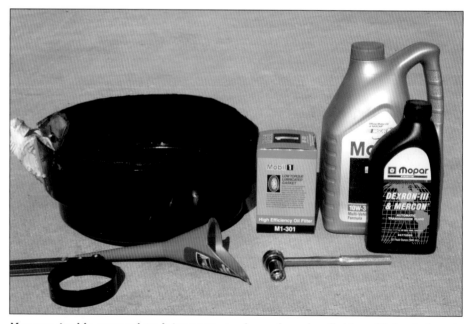

You can tackle general maintenance, such as changing fluids, with basic hand tools in your driveway. The more you do yourself, the more familiar you become with your vehicle.

Technical automotive manuals are a great resource. The Haynes manual on the left is a good start for general maintenance, but even though it states it covers 1984 to 2000, it is more specific for the older XJs before 1995 or so. The factory service manual is much more detailed. Even though it covers just one model year, it's almost three times as thick as the Haynes.

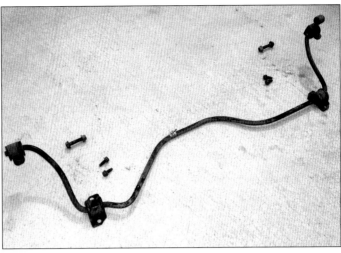

The sway bar helps limit body roll in the corners, but it will also limit how much the suspension can flex when off-road. Removing the rear sway bar is an easy modification that can make a big difference for your stock XJ.

Maintaining your own vehicle can be very beneficial. Not only do you save money by not having to pay someone else to do the work, but the knowledge you gain about your vehicle is invaluable. By doing it yourself, you know exactly what has been done and that the work is done to your standards. Remember the old adage: If you want something done right, do it yourself.

The how-tos of general maintenance aren't covered in this book; that could be a book by itself. In fact, your local auto-parts store probably sells Cherokee-specific repair manuals for less than $20. These manuals are good at teaching most basic procedures such as changing the oil or working on the brakes. But for a more comprehensive and detailed manual specific to your year of Cherokee, nothing beats the factory service manual.

For modifications, doing it yourself is even more valuable because you are able to diagnose problems as they occur and have a better chance of fixing them. Of course nobody expects

you to jump in and start setting up gears or rebuilding engines, but you'd be surprised once you learn how easy many of the modifications actually are to perform. Even most lift kits can be installed with a set of decent hand tools in your garage or driveway. Most of all, you can be proud of your work. There is another saying that goes: Real Jeeps are built, not bought!

Beginning Modifications: Sway Bar Removal

Removing the rear sway bar is one of the most common first mod-

ifications made to a stock Cherokee. With the exception of the Up Country package, all XJs have a front and rear sway bar. XJs with the Up Country package have no rear sway bar due to slightly stiffer leaf springs that have about 1 inch of lift from the factory. The more correct name for a sway bar is "anti-sway bar" or "stabilizer bar," because its purpose is to limit body roll, keeping the vehicle from leaning too much when it turns. The sway bars are a safety feature designed to decrease the risk of rollovers and to provide better handling. Even though "sway bar"

This shows the before (left) and after (right) shots of how much more I could stuff the tire up into the fenderwell after I removed the sway bar.

On the other side of the Jeep, I measured 1 inch of increased droop between the tire and the flare after sway bar removal. I know it doesn't sound like much, but keeping your tires planted means traction and stability, and every little bit helps.

is the less technically correct term, it is the most common, so I use it throughout this book.

So why would you want to remove an important safety feature? The answer is to gain more wheel travel, or articulation, from the suspension. In order to limit body roll, the sway bar is designed to keep the axle parallel to the body. For off-road driving over uneven terrain, this often causes one or more wheels to rise off the ground. When a wheel is not touching the ground, it isn't providing any traction. Without a traction device such as a locker, when one wheel is raised up, all power goes to that wheel instead of the wheel still on the ground, which needs it most. Removing the rear sway bar allows the axle to droop further, keeping the tires on the ground as much as possible.

Now that you understand the benefits of removing the rear sway bar for off-road use, you might still be wondering if it is safe to drive on the street. It is safe to permanently remove the rear sway bar, with a few caveats. First and foremost, you should drive the Jeep like a Jeep and not a sports car. If you feel the need to take turns unreasonably fast, you should probably keep the sway bar on. Most people notice little to no difference in the way their Jeep handles with the rear sway bar removed. If you remove it and don't like how it feels, you can always reinstall it. The other caveat is for towing. If you plan on towing with the XJ, it's recommended that you leave the rear sway bar on as a precaution.

The front sway bar should always remain connected for on-road use. In the event of an emergency, the lack of a front sway bar may cause you to lose control of the vehicle. Some people feel that it's okay to run without a front sway bar at all, and they justify their decision by using very stiff shocks in the front. For off-road use, you can disconnect the front sway bar and temporarily secure it out of the way using a bungee cord, zip tie, or special strap. There are several companies that offer "quick disconnects" to make disconnecting and reconnecting the sway bar a painless procedure.

With quick disconnects, the front sway bar can be disconnected and secured out of the way for off-road use.

Removing the Rear Sway Bar

1 Park the Jeep on a level surface and block the front wheels. With the floor jack positioned securely under the rear axle, raise the jack and remove both rear wheels. Place jack stands under the frame rails as shown and lower the jack part way until the weight of the vehicle is on the stands but the rear axle is still supported by the jack.

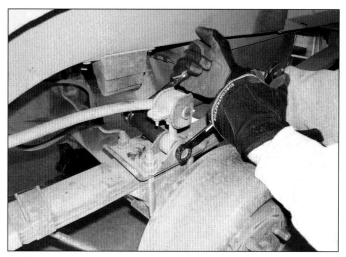

2 Remove the nut and bolt that connects the sway bar to the leaf-spring plate using an 18-mm socket and wrench.

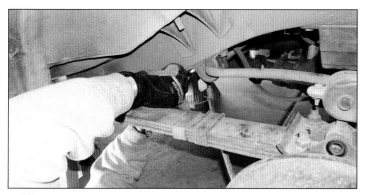

3 Using a 15-mm socket or wrench, remove the two bolts that hold the sway bar to the bottom of the frame rail.

4 After the sway bar bolts are removed from both sides, lower the rear axle with the jack to create more room to pull the sway bar out.

6 Discard the sway bar, unless you are one of those guys who suffers from "separation anxiety" when you remove something from your Jeep and can't bring yourself to ever throw it away!

5 Raise the axle back up as needed to put the wheels back on. Raise it farther to remove the jack stands and then lower the Jeep to the ground. Make sure the lug nuts on the wheels are tight enough. It's a good idea to check them again after a couple of days.

Jeep XJ Profile: Travis Thompson's 1988 XJ

Travis Thompson built his XJ for Nevada's desert terrain. It has a 3-inch Old Man Emu suspension and 31-inch BFG All-Terrain tires.

Year: 1988
Engine: 4.0L I-6
Transmission: BA10/5 Peugeot 5-speed manual
Transfer case: NP231 w/HD SYE
Front axle: Dana 30
Rear axle: Dana 44
Gears: 4.56:1
Lockers: Limited slips, front and rear
Steering: Stock drag link, RE HD tie-rod
Suspension: 3-inch mixed lift
Shocks: Old Man Emu
Tires: 31 x 10.50–inch BFG A/T
Wheels: Stock 15 x 7–inch from a 1997 XJ

Travis built this XJ mostly for Nevada's desert terrain. It's low to the ground with just a 3-inch lift. The stock wheels and 31-inch tires are proportional to the lift, so it looks stock until it's sitting next to an actual stock XJ. The suspension consists of 2.5-inch Old Man Emu coils with a 1-inch coil spacer in the front, and 2.5-inch Old Man Emu leafs with shackles from an MJ Comanche in the back for an additional 3/4-inch lift. The control arms are from Rubicon Express, and he's running a JKS track bar.

Even though it wasn't built with the intent to tackle very rocky trails, Travis finds himself in the rocks more and more now and has even taken this XJ through the Rubicon twice. That wouldn't have been possible without the extensive custom work he's done to beef up and protect his rig. He has reinforced his stock crossmember with steel diamond plate to make it indestructible (his buckling frame rails are proof of that!). He also has a beefed-up front skid and a custom reinforced front differential cover. His custom-built rock rails see a lot of use, and his rear tube bumper with built-in quarter panel and taillight guards work very well keeping them out of harm's way.

To play in the rocks, you need good protection. You can tell by the amount of rock rash on Travis's rails that they are well used. Travis built his rock rails and tube bumpers himself.

Travis is not easy on his rig, and I've witnessed him do some stuff on 31s that was nothing short of amazing. The very first time we went wheeling together, it was getting dark and Travis was maneuvering his XJ through a difficult section of trail. He nudged a very large boulder with his front bumper; the rock came loose from the wall and rested against the side of his Jeep. Travis kept going and that boulder caused lots of neat carnage on his rig! It dented both doors, tore off both door handles, and broke the rear side window. About two weeks later, Travis showed up to the next run with the damage almost completely repaired except for some ripples in the doors. Oh, and that boulder that did the damage? We named it *The Travis Rock*. Travis has proved that you don't need a lot of lift to do difficult trails, as long as you have your XJ well protected and aren't afraid of picking up some damage. Travis knows that the unibody may not stand up to his abuse, so one of his future modifications will likely be swapping into a fresh unibody. ∎

Rocky trails like this can be challenging for XJs with smaller tires. Travis makes it through this section with ease.

Making it over a tough obstacle like this not only takes some help from traction aids such as front and rear limited-slip differentials, but also a good amount of driver skill.

SUSPENSION UPGRADES

The suspension is a vital part of any off-road vehicle. The quality and design of the suspension largely affects how your Jeep handles both on- and off-road. The XJ's stock suspension consists of coil springs up front and leaf springs in the rear. A leaf-spring suspension is very basic compared to a coil-spring setup. The XJ's rear suspension consists of only the leaf springs, shackle, and shocks (after you removed that sway bar, of course). On the other hand, the front suspension uses coil springs, a track bar, four control arms, shocks, and the sway bar.

The purpose of the springs, whether coils or leafs, is to support the body on the axles and isolate it from the road. They also keep the tires planted on the road. The shocks dampen the spring's compression and rebound movement. Without the shocks, the ride would be very bouncy. The four control arms locate the front axle front to rear, and the track bar keeps the axle centered side to side under the body. With the rear suspension, the leaf springs locate the axle (as well as acting as the springs), so there is no need for control arms or a track bar.

Because changes to the front suspension can affect the align-

The suspension is one of the most important systems on an off-road vehicle. It not only provides lift to raise the vehicle, but it also affects how the vehicle will handle in off-road terrain. One goal of the suspension is to keep the tires on the ground as much as possible. When a wheel lifts off the ground, traction is lost. (Photo Courtesy Jason West)

ment and steering, there is a greater chance for things to go wrong if you don't do things right when you lift it. Luckily, several companies offer lift kits, most of which are bolt-on, that, when installed properly, retain or even improve driveability on the street. Of course, a properly designed

lift kit also greatly improves the suspension performance of your XJ as it crawls over rocks or other challenging off-road terrain.

When selecting a lift kit, there are a few basic things you must first consider, and understanding why a lift is needed helps you choose the

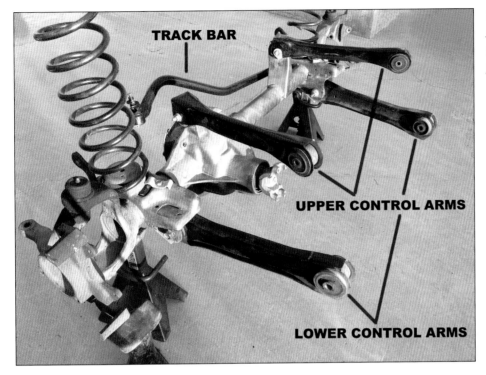

TRACK BAR

UPPER CONTROL ARMS

LOWER CONTROL ARMS

This is a mock-up of the stock front suspension. It shows the location of the four control arms and the track bar in front of the axle.

right kit for your needs. A lift accomplishes two things: It gives you clearance under the belly of your XJ and allows room for bigger tires. You need bigger tires for more clearance under the axles. As far as lift height is concerned, bigger isn't always better, because going taller raises the center of gravity, which might actually make your Jeep less stable and more tippy in off-camber situations. In addition, the taller you go, the more issues you have to address in the driveline and steering. A good combination of lift and fender trimming can give you clearance for bigger tires. Ideally, you should choose your suspension height based on what tire size you want to run. If you don't already know what tire size you want, make sure you read the other chapters that discuss tires, axles, and driveline before you decide which lift kit to buy.

Now, before I discuss different lift kits, let me briefly address one commonly asked question from new Cherokee owners: "Can I do a body lift on my XJ?" The answer is no, you cannot do a body lift on an XJ. A body lift raises the body up from the frame. But since the XJ uses unibody construction, you cannot separate the body from the frame. Although it is true that the XJ is lacking a traditional frame, it does have thinner frame rails that are part of the unibody.

2-Inch Budget Boost

A "budget boost" usually refers to a lift kit that affordably lifts the XJ 1.5 to 2 inches. Very few parts are involved in a budget boost, so it is usually easy to install and inex-

pensive, hence the name. Most lift kits in this range use a coil spacer (usually 1.75 inches thick) inserted between the coil springs and the body. Because the stock coil springs are retained, you can expect that the handling does not change much from the stock height.

There are three common ways that budget boosts lift the rear. One way is by replacing the stock leaf-spring shackle with a taller one. You can also insert an add-a-leaf (AAL) into the stock leaf pack (if this method is used, I recommend a long AAL, which supports the stock leaf pack better than a short AAL). The third method is to insert a block between the leaf pack and the axle. Depending on which method is used to lift the rear, the handling may or may not be affected. Using the extended shackle, you can expect little change in the way it rides. If you choose the AAL, you definitely notice a change because most AALs stiffen the leaf pack considerably. Whether that stiffness is a change for the better or worse is subject to personal opinion. Using blocks can sometimes lead to axle wrap, especially if you have a heavy right foot. Axle wrap is when the leaf springs flex into an

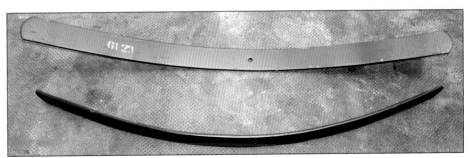

Add-a-leafs are a single leaf added to an existing leaf pack, to give it more lift.

Extended shackles are used to gain lift in the back. This is the stock shackle compared to a TeraFlex 1.75-inch shackle.

You can insert coil spacers between the coil springs and the body to give the front end a little lift. Shown here is a TeraFlex 1.5-inch spacer with the stock isolator (the rubber pad cushioning the coil against the body) removed. To gain the full amount of lift with a coil spacer, use it with the stock isolator.

"S" shape under heavy acceleration. This can cause adverse effects such as driveline vibration when the bending leafs push the pinion upward.

There are other ways to piece together a 2-inch lift. Coil springs out of a ZJ Grand Cherokee with the V-8 engine lift your XJ about 2 inches. Junkyard leaf springs can be used as AALs for the rear. XJ leafs are 2.5 inches wide, so it is possible to use individual leafs from other vehicles such as the Dodge Dakota or Chevy S-10. If you have a spare set of XJ leaf springs available, the main leaf can be used as an AAL by cutting the ends off and adding it to your spring pack. This is probably better than using non-XJ leafs because the XJ AAL has the same spring rate as the rest of your leafs. The second and third leafs could also be used as AALs. Shackles from an MJ Comanche also net approximately 3/4-inch lift when used on an XJ.

A budget boost is a good lift for the novice do-it-yourselfer who is hesitant about trying a taller lift for fear that he might mess up something during the installation. Because of the relative simplicity of a budget boost, if you are unhappy with the results, it can be easily removed and the vehicle returned to stock height.

A 2-inch budget boost can fit 30 x 9.50–inch tires without fender trimming, but you can fit 31s if you are willing to trim. Budget boost kits can be obtained from many of the companies that sell taller lift kits, such as Rubicon Express, Rusty's Off-Road, TeraFlex, and others.

Although a 2-inch budget boost makes your XJ more capable, don't expect it to turn your XJ into the ultimate off-roader. An experienced driver in a stock XJ can out-wheel most novice drivers with a budget boost, but that's true even for taller lifts.

The 3-inch lift kits are very popular entry-level lifts, and with 31-inch tires on stock wheels, you need very little modification to the body or flares. The owner of this older-body-style 1988 has trimmed away the front fender so that it is level with the headlights. This is recommended, but not always necessary, with "small" tires such as 31s.

3-Inch Lift Kits

Three-inch lift kits are popular as entry-level lifts for many Cherokee owners. A typical 3-inch lift kit replaces the stock coils with taller aftermarket coils. Many kits include full replacement leaf packs or a 3-inch AAL as a cheaper alternative for the rear. Using full replacement leaf packs is better than trying to make do with an old, tired, rusty stock leaf pack and AAL. You get not only all new leafs, but new bushings as well. Kits that include aftermarket control arms are always good, as the aftermarket pieces are much stronger than the stock control arms. Aftermarket control arms with high-performance flex joints also

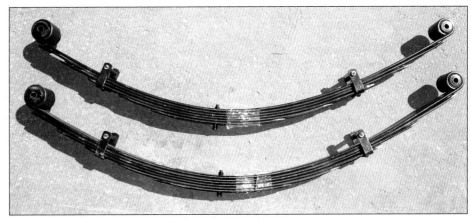

Replacement leaf packs are better than using add-a-leafs (AAL) in most cases. These are Rubicon Express 4.5-inch leaf packs.

allow more articulation than simple rubber bushings.

With 3 inches of lift, brake-line length should be watched, especially in the rear. Brake lines that are too short may be ripped out as the suspension flexes. Some taller kits replace the stock lines with longer, braided stainless steel lines. For kits that do not include extended brake

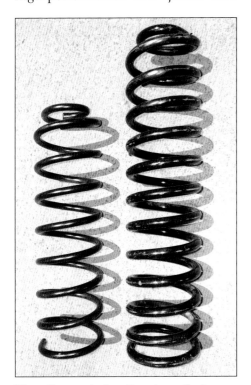

The aftermarket coil springs that come in lift kits are taller than stock, and the coil itself is a thicker diameter. The coil's thickness and how tightly it is wound determine its spring rate. Most aftermarket coils have higher spring rates than stock.

The hard brake line can be straightened by hand and relocated for additional length. This photo shows the brake line mounted 2 inches lower than its original location on the frame rail. The white line shows the original position of the brake line before it was straightened.

lines, the stock hard lines for the front brakes can be straightened out by hand and re-attached lower in the fenderwell. This usually provides enough slack in the line so it isn't ripped out.

You also need longer shocks with a 3-inch lift, but many kits do not include them. This is helpful because you can choose which shocks you want, rather than be limited to whatever brand comes as part of the kit. The lift-kit company can tell you what length shocks you need and give brand recommendations if you are unsure about what you want.

A wide range of 3-inch kits is available, but not all of them include the same parts. A typical 3-inch kit includes the following parts:

- 3-inch front coil springs
- 3-inch rear leaf packs or AAL/shackle
- Lower control arms
- Shocks
- U-bolts
- Extended sway bar links
- Extended rear brake line
- Transfer case lowering kit (optional)

Lift Installation Tips

Small lifts like a "budget boost" can usually be installed with basic hand tools. A floor jack and jack stands are mandatory. Deep sockets and a breaker bar will really help you out. It's also much easier with a helper.

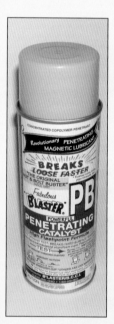

Every day for at least a week prior to the install, you should lubricate every bolt that will be removed. PB Blaster is a penetrating lubricant that works very well to free rusted bolts. It can be found at auto parts stores or Wal-Mart. This should save you some time and effort on the big day.

Power tools, especially a drill and angle grinder, should be considered mandatory for taller lifts. Don't be surprised when parts don't fit as they should; that's when the power tools really come in handy.

- Extended bumpstops (optional)
- Track-bar relocation bracket (optional)

How elaborate a kit you choose will be based on your budget and personal preference. So, do you need all the extra parts that some kits have and others don't? You may or may not. My personal opinion is that you don't need to relocate the track bar for a 3-inch kit, and you might not need the transfer-case lowering kit, either. Aftermarket control arms are also preferred at this height, but not absolutely necessary. However, I do think the extended rear brake line and new U-bolts should be high priorities, and longer sway bar disconnects are a good idea. Those parts could be purchased separately if not included in the kit of your choice.

A 3-inch lift kit with 31 x 10.50–inch tires is a popular combo. Bigger tires can be used with fender trimming. Even though 3-inch lift kits are mild as far as lift height is concerned, an XJ with a 3-inch lift and 31s can be a very capable trail rig and still be very practical as a daily driver.

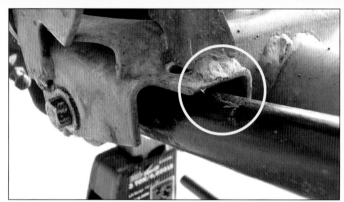

You can see that there isn't much room above the track bar before it makes contact with the mount on the axle. Grinding away some of the metal above the track bar will improve your flex by giving it more room to move upward before it binds.

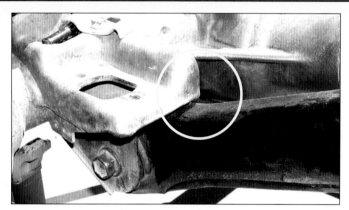

Stock lower control arms (LCAs) often make contact with the bracket (as shown here). You can grind away quite a bit of metal for more clearance; just don't take off too much, because that's where the shocks mount. Many aftermarket LCAs don't have this problem.

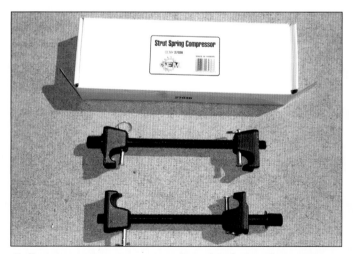

Coil spring compressors can be a big help when removing or installing springs from the vehicle. You can borrow them from AutoZone with a refundable deposit (they are PN 27036 and labeled "Strut Spring Compressor").

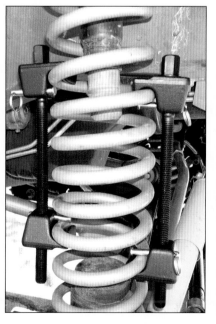

This photo shows how the spring compressors fit on the coil spring. Start by lowering the axle as far as possible, and then compress the spring until you can remove it from the Jeep. Be careful when handling a compressed spring. If it suddenly unloads, it can become a deadly projectile.

This Rubicon Express Super-Flex joint will allow the arm to articulate much more than will stock rubber bushings.

One word of caution: Many people find that after installing their first lift kit they soon have the urge to go even higher. Working your way up with different lift heights is a good way to get experience, but it almost always costs you more in the long run than going with a taller kit from the beginning. Because upgrad-

ing with another lift kit is expensive, many people look to cheaper methods of increasing lift height. Adding coil spacers and extended shackles to your 3-inch lift does work, but make sure you address the same issues that people with taller lifts have to deal with, such as the track bar, brake-line length, shock length, and driveline angles.

4- to 6-Inch Lift Kits

At 4 to 6 inches of lift, control-arm angles start to become an issue and adversely affect ride quality. With a short-arm suspension, the taller the lift, the steeper the control arms in relation to the ground. This results in a harsher ride, since bumps and jolts can travel up the arms to the body. Control arms that are in a more horizontal position allow the bumps to be absorbed more by the springs and shocks.

Another thing to be aware of is that the steeper the control-arm angle, the farther the front wheel is pulled to the rear of the front wheel-well. This often has no negative effect other than how it looks. In other cases, it may result in fender rubbing when turning and/or the coils bowing slightly forward.

On any lift 4 inches or taller, track bar length is an issue. The taller the body is lifted, the more the stock track bar pulls the front axle over to the driver's side. The track bar's job is to keep the axle centered under the vehicle, so in order to keep the axle centered, the track bar must either be lengthened or repositioned. Some people drill a new hole in the axle mount to reposition it, but there isn't a lot of metal to work with in that area. Besides, even if you can get the axle centered with the stock track bar, it doesn't flex as well as an aftermarket bar because it was meant for an XJ with no lift. The best option is to replace the stock track bar with an aftermarket adjustable track bar that can be set to the correct length and operates properly when flexing.

At around 6 inches of lift, some XJs with the low-pinion front axle (2000–2001) might have problems with front driveshaft angle. Adjustable control arms can be used to rotate the pinion more in-line with the front driveshaft, but rotating the pinion up reduces the amount of caster, which is a crucial part of the alignment. Not to worry though; XJs with short-arm suspensions in the 4- to 6-inch range are common, and the Jeep can still handle well as a daily driver. *Project Rubicon's* first suspension lift was the Rubicon Express 4.5-inch lift kit, with a 3/4-inch coil spacer added. It sat between 5 and 5.5 inches. Even with this short-arm

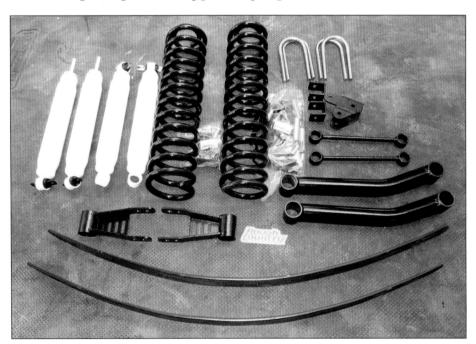

This is the Rough Country 4.5-inch lift kit with AALs. The taller the lift kit, the more complex it becomes, hence the additional parts and hardware. Using AALs will be cheaper than full leaf packs, but, in the long run, kits in this height range will be better off with full replacement leaf packs.

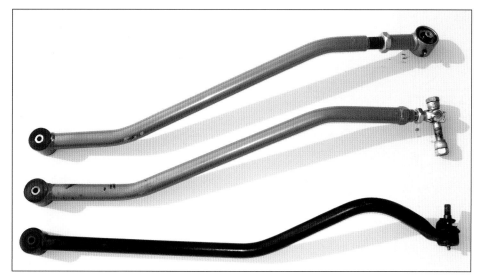

Here are different track bars that can be used to keep the axle centered under the body. The one at the bottom is a stock track bar. The Rubicon Express 1600 adjustable track bar with Heim joint (middle) is recommended for 3 to 4 inches of lift. The Rubicon Express 1660 adjustable track bar with a Super-Flex joint (top) is recommended for 4 to 6 inches of lift and requires a different bracket that mounts to the frame.

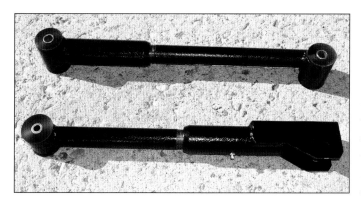

These adjustable control arms by Rough Country can be lengthened or shortened. When installed, these arms are also left free to twist for better articulation.

suspension, *Project Rubicon* handled very well on the street. Off-road, the 4.5-inch suspension performed well and offered plenty of flex.

The Rubicon Express 4.5-inch Super-Flex kit is a good example of a complete 4.5-inch lift kit.

Rubicon Express 4.5-Inch Super-Flex Kit

- 4.5-inch front coil springs
- 3.5-inch rear leaf spring packs
- 1.25-inch extended shackle
- Lower control arms
- Upper control arms
- Track bar (3-inch +)
- Sway bar disconnects
- 2-inch front bumpstops
- Extended front brake lines
- Extended rear brake line
- U-bolts
- Transfer case lowering kit

Project Rubicon's first lift was the Rubicon Express (RE) 4.5-inch kit. At the time, I chose to use RE's 4.5-inch leaf packs instead of the 3.5-inch leaf packs and extended shackle. This was not the wisest decision because the 4.5-inch leaf packs netted me between 5 and 5.5 inches after they settled. I added 3/4-inch coil spacers to the front to level the Jeep. I found that the stock shackle was preventing the 4.5-inch leafs from flexing as much as they should, and this resulted in a stiff rear suspension. Using the 3.5-inch leaf packs with an extended shackle would have flexed better off-road.

Even though RE advertises that its extended shackle provides 1.25 inches of lift; in reality it only gives

Longer sway bar links are needed for lifts of 3 inches or more. These "quick disconnects" from JKS make disconnecting for the trail easy. The rubber bushings also prevent clunking that occurs with other types of disconnects.

7/8 inch. A shackle's lift height is determined by measuring its length from the center of the eyes, subtracting the length of the stock shackle, and dividing by 2. I don't know how RE came up with the 1.25-inch figure, but taking detailed measurements of several different shackles and comparing them with the RE shackle confirmed that it does not provide 1.25 inches of lift. Regardless, this shackle works very well with the 4.5-inch lift kit. The leaf packs should give slightly more than 3.5 inches, so with the RE shackle giving 7/8-inch lift, most people get close to the advertised height of 4.5 inches.

Long-Arm Suspensions

With taller lift heights, especially in the 6-inch range or taller, many people prefer a long-arm kit over a short-arm. Much of this is due to the steep control-arm angles that I mentioned above with the short-arms. Because long-arms attach farther back along the frame rail, their angle is reduced, greatly improving the ride and, in many cases, offering better flex than a short-arm suspension. A long-arm suspension can have disadvantages as well. Depending on how the long-arms mount to the frame rails, they may cause a loss of ground clearance since they are mounted farther back toward the center of the Jeep.

One alternative to long-arms is control-arm drop brackets from Rubicon Express. These are included in the Rubicon Express 5.5-inch HD short-arm lift kit. The drop brackets lower both upper and lower control arms 4 inches from their original mounting points on the body. The drop brackets come paired with support braces that are essential to

Long-arm kits are becoming increasingly popular. They offer a much better ride on the street and can flex better than most short-arm suspensions.

One disadvantage of long-arms is that most of them mount to the bottom of the frame rail toward the center of the Jeep. This loss of ground clearance sometimes hurts, so the arms must be able to handle the abuse if used in the rocks. These TeraFlex long-arms have beefy modular joints on both ends.

maintaining the integrity of the control-arm mounts. I have noticed a big improvement in the way the Jeep handles and flexes after installing these on *Project Rubicon*. However, it still isn't a perfect setup because the

drop brackets give up clearance as well. They often make contact after my front wheel comes down off a big rock, but the drop brackets and braces are made to handle the abuse. The same situations would also

The white line in this photo shows the angle of the control arm without the drop brackets. The steeper the control-arm angle, the harsher the ride will be.

Drop brackets also allow for better flex when everything else is set properly. Notice that the coil has become unseated from the body by 2 or 3 inches. At this point, the shock is preventing the axle from drooping farther, but since the weight of the vehicle is not pushing down on that side of the axle, having it droop more won't give that tire any more traction. Also note that the brake line is not stretched tight, even with this amount of droop.

likely scrape the control arms on a long-arm suspension.

Choosing which suspension is best for you should largely depend on the type of terrain. Even for rocks, some people swear by long-arm suspensions. In some cases, a mid-arm suspension might be the best of both worlds, but as of this writing, the only lift kits on the market that could be considered mid-arm suspensions are the 6- and 8-inch kits made by Skyjacker. The Skyjacker kits for the XJ have been available for several years, even before the big long-arm craze began. These kits are still considered pretty good, except for the small Heim joints used on both ends of the control arms. Many people with these kits are swapping in larger Heim joints.

Another type of long-arm suspension modification that has become popular is the radius-arm kit. Rubicon Express, Rough Country, and T&T Customs are some companies that offer these kits. The T&T Customs Y-Link kit includes a very beefy belly pan that replaces the stock crossmember, doubles as a transfer case skid, and includes a built-in 1-inch transfer-case drop. Instead of mounting the arms to the bottom of the frame rails, T&T Customs integrated the control-arm mounts with

The T&T Customs long-arm kit includes the belly pan and control arms. It can be used with whichever coils and rear suspension you want.

The huge benefit to the T&T kit is that the arms mount to the belly pan and are tucked higher up to the inside of the frame rails. There is no loss of clearance compared to other long-arms that mount to the bottom of the frame rail.

the belly pan. The result is a long-arm kit that doesn't give up any clearance underneath the frame rails, and the upward bend of the arms extends that added clearance all the way to the front axle. Installing this kit involves a lot of drilling into the frame rails, which can be very tedious, but T&T Customs wanted to keep it a bolt-on kit rather than a welded-on kit. The numerous mounting points for the belly pan provide a very strong foundation for the long-arms, creating a system that handles the stress of driving in extreme off-road terrain.

Achieving a Balanced Suspension

Because the XJ has both coils and leaf springs, achieving a balanced suspension can be a challenge sometimes, especially once it's lifted. Most often, the front coil suspension has a large amount of flex and the rear leaf springs are rather stiff. This can lead to some uncomfortable situations on the trail when the body of the Jeep stays relatively parallel with the rear axle on sloped terrain. A balanced suspension with equal amounts of articulation front and rear helps keep the body level and lets the axles follow the slopes of the terrain. The reason the rear suspension tends to be stiffer is because aftermarket leaf packs that provide lift naturally have more arch to them.

On the other hand, flat leafs flex more easily, but it's hard to gain any lift by using flat leafs! In my experience, any leaf pack that adds 4 inches or more needs an extended shackle in order to flex properly. Using the stock shackle with a leaf pack with a lot of arch is stiffer because the short shackle does not allow the leafs to flatten out when the suspension tries to compress.

Achieving a balanced suspension isn't always a big concern with most people, unless they have a very unbalanced suspension to begin with. I feel that knowing about the

The MJ Comanche's front end is almost identical to the XJ's. The owner of this MJ did a front leaf spring conversion at the same time that he swapped in the full-width axles.

situation beforehand might be beneficial to you. Probably the best way to balance a Cherokee's suspension is to do away with the coil/leaf combination. Some people do rear coil conversions or front leaf spring conversions. Although this gives you a balanced suspension, these types of conversions are rarely done for just this reason. There can be other advantages and disadvantages, so they aren't for everyone. Here are some tips to improve your coil/leaf suspension:

- Use coil springs with a higher spring rate than the stock coils (most aftermarket coils are higher).
- Avoid using stock shackles with leaf packs that have a lot of arch.
- Using a greaseable shackle may help.
- Use shackle relocation brackets.
- Use Teflon pads between the leafs to reduce friction (most aftermarket leaf packs include them).
- If repainting the leafs, some people have used Teflon paint with good results.

- Properly extend bumpstops to control where the springs stop compressing.

- Try to load the vehicle evenly. Too much weight front or rear affects the suspension.

This is John Laurella's XJ with a long-arm front coil suspension and rear leaf springs. Typical of most XJs, the front suspension is doing all the work. John's goal is to get as much flex in the back as he has up front. The following photos detail his rear coil-over conversion. (Photo Courtesy John Laurella)

A new Dana 60 differential cover and truss from Blue Torch Fab will provide the axle mounts for the new upper control arms. (Photo Courtesy John Laurella)

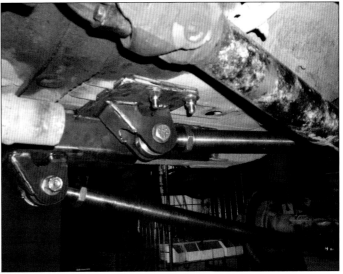

The frame rails are sleeved and control-arm mounts are fabricated. (Photo Courtesy John Laurella)

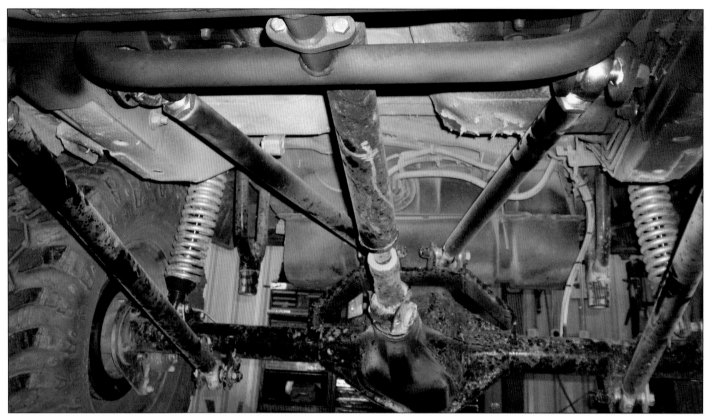

This shows the geometry of John's four-link suspension. The upper arms are triangulated, which eliminates the need for a track bar. (Photo Courtesy John Laurella)

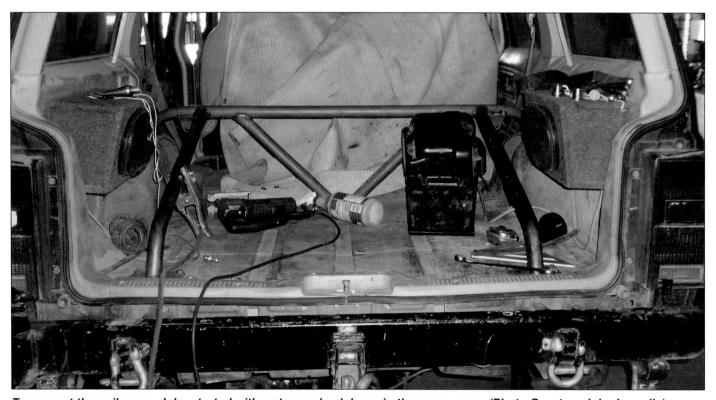

To support the coil-overs, John started with a strong shock hoop in the cargo area. (Photo Courtesy John Laurella)

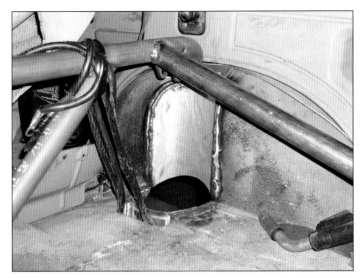

John's plans were to use coil-overs with 14 inches of travel. The length of the coil-overs required mounting them inside the XJ. This photo shows the modifications to the floor and wheel well to create the opening. (Photo Courtesy John Laurella)

Here is the coil-over mounted to the shock hoop. The shocks are 2-inch-body RaceRunners from Sway-A-Way and have a remote reservoir (strapped to the hoop). These shocks have 14 inches of travel, hence the need to mount them through the floor. (Photo Courtesy John Laurella)

The result is a balanced suspension. Notice how the body is level yet both front and rear axles are articulated equally in opposite directions. (Photo Courtesy John Laurella)

Off-road coil-overs typically have two coils for each shock. With these, the lower coil has a higher spring rate than the upper. The suspension can be tuned just right by selecting the proper spring rates and shock valving for the vehicle. (Photo Courtesy John Laurella)

Rear Coil-Over Conversion

John Laurella decided that to balance his suspension, he would replace his leaf springs with a custom four-link coil-over suspension. The term "four-link" refers to the four control arms that are used to locate the rear axle. And "coil-overs" are a shock and coil-spring combination; the shock is inside the coil. This is different from an average rear coil conversion, and in some ways much easier. Coil-overs take up less room because the shock is inside the coil.

Coil-overs are much more than just shocks with coils on them. They are highly customizable: different coils with different spring rates and shocks with adjustable valving. The coil-over setup needs to be tuned specifically to the vehicle, according to variables including vehicle weight and its intended use (rock crawling versus pre-runner racing). The spring

RTI ramps are used to test a vehicle's ability to flex, but they're also used to make sure the shocks, brake lines, and bumpstops are set to the right length. You can see that John has an incredible amount of articulation in the rear suspension. He is planning on adding limiting straps to control how much the axles droop. Sometimes it's possible to have too much of a good thing! (Photo Courtesy John Laurella)

rates and shock valving used on John's XJ may be very different from that necessary for yours. Outer Limit Motorsports of Salt Lake City, Utah, set up this conversion. The photos on pages 35 to 39 show John's coil-over project on his XJ, *The Badger*.

Shocks

The purpose of the shocks is to dampen the movement of the suspension. Without shocks, the body would bounce several times after going over each bump. The shocks resist suspension movement according to how soft or stiff they are. Shocks that are valved too soft or are worn out do not dampen adequately and give you a bouncy ride. On the other hand, shocks that are too stiff give you a rigid ride.

Several types of shocks are available for specific driving applications, each providing various degrees of ride comfort. Ultimately, the type of shock you use is according to your likes and dislikes. Twin-tube shocks are usually inexpensive entry-level hydraulic shocks. Monotube and gas-pressurized shocks are built better and offer more consistent dampening than twin-tubes. Usually, gas shocks are stiffer than most hydraulic shocks, but some are valved for specific vehicles or suspensions by the manufacturer. Rancho even offers an adjustable gas shock: the RS9000 series. There are also shocks with remote reservoirs designed more for off-road racing applications.

Along with deciding the type of shocks to buy, you also need to make sure they are the correct length. Most often it is the shocks that limit the downward travel of the suspension, so shocks that are too short greatly reduce the amount of flex. Shocks that are too long bottom out on compression, possibly causing damage to the shock or shock mounts.

Extended bumpstops should always be used if there is a risk of the shocks bottoming out.

This is a Bilstein 5150 shock. It is a nitrogen-gas-charged monotube shock with an added fixed reservoir. (Photo Courtesy Jason West)

Jason West is testing Big Red on an RTI ramp. (Photo Courtesy Jason West)

So what length shocks do you need? Ideally, the best way to make sure you select the correct length is to hold off on buying the shocks until after the lift is installed. (This may be impractical if the Jeep is your daily driver.) Then test the flex on an RTI ramp or large rock. RTI stands for ramp travel index and gives a score for how much your vehicle can flex. You don't need to calculate your Jeep's RTI score (unless you want to) but you need to know how much up-travel and down-travel the suspension has. Measuring the distance between the shock mounts, you know the ideal length of shocks needed to match your suspension.

Without testing the flex first, you have to rely on the shock or lift-kit manufacturer to tell you what length works. If you're lucky, they recommend shocks that are just what you need, but in many cases, the recommended shocks are a little short or a little long. Of course, you need to factor in bumpstop lengths and how much adjustment you want to add, or return the shocks for the correct size and just use trial and error.

If you want to calculate your RTI score, the formula is:

$$\text{RTI Score} = \text{distance driven up ramp} \div \text{wheelbase} \times 1{,}000$$

Post-Lift Maintenance

The first thing you need after you install your lift is an alignment. Any time the suspension height is altered, the alignment (particularly the toe setting) is also affected. Even though the Jeep may track perfectly straight going down the road, without correcting the alignment, the tires wear away very fast. It's nice to have the alignment done pro-fessionally because the shop can provide you with a printout that lists the before-and-after toe, caster, and camber measurements. This could be valuable information later on if you're trying to troubleshoot front-end problems.

You'll notice that after the lift, your Jeep handles differently on the road. More often than not, the ride is stiffer due to the coils having a higher spring rate and the leafs having more arch. It may feel more truck-like now, and with a higher center of gravity, it should be driven like the lifted Jeep that it is, not like a sports car.

It's also normal for the lifted ride height to be slightly more than the amount of advertised lift. Most lift-kit manufacturers realize that Jeeps built for off-road are heavier than stock due to beefy aftermarket bumpers, skid plates, winches, spare parts, and tools. They factor in this weight when designing lift kits and spring rates. Loading the rear of the Jeep with some heavy items will help the leaf packs settle in, usually dropping 1/2 to 1 inch over the next few months. Frequent suspension flexing also helps it settle.

When flexing the suspension for the first time, you should check that the brake lines are long enough and positioned in a safe area (not making contact with the tire!). Also check that the control arms, track bar, and steering parts are not binding. When flexed, you can also see if the bumpstops need to be extended farther or if more fender trimming is needed.

Don't be surprised if new clunks and squeaks develop after a short time. Sway bar disconnects are a common cause of front-end clunking, but it could also be from a loose part somewhere. All bolts, particularly the track bar and control arms, should be checked and retightened if needed. Also, after each off-road trip, get into the habit of doing regular inspections for damaged and loose

You can adjust your toe setting by lengthening or shortening the tie-rod, but an alignment shop can be much more precise.

Jeep XJ Profile: Lee Harper's 2001 XJ

Lee's 2001 XJ features a Maggiolina rooftop tent, a rear bumper and tire carrier by Custom 4x4 Fabrication, and BushWacker flares covering 33-inch Goodyear MT/R tires.

Year: 2001
Engine: 4.0L I-6
Transmission: AW 4-speed
Transfer Case: NP242 + SYE
Front Axle: LP Dana 30
Rear Axle: Chrysler 8.25
Gears: 4.56:1
Lockers: ARB front and rear
Steering: Stock with ZJ pitman arm
Suspension: RE 5.5-inch Extreme Duty short-arm
Shocks: Rancho 9000
Tires: 33 x 12.50–inch Goodyear MT/R
Wheels: 15 x 8–inch Tech 1 Rockcrawlers

Lee Harper built his XJ for one reason: expeditions. For many years, Lee and his wife have enjoyed exploring some of the most remote areas of the world, visiting ancient Indian habitats and rock-art sites. Many of his journeys are in the Great Basin of North America, which includes Utah, Nevada, and parts of Idaho. His XJ has taken them to Oaxaca, Mexico, where they saw the ruins of Monte Alban, and other even more obscure sites.

So why did Lee choose the Jeep Cherokee as an expedition vehicle? Let me start at the beginning. Lee drove a Nissan pickup for about 10 years, but he came to find that it couldn't take him to all the places he wanted to go. Like all pickup trucks, the departure angle was horrible, yet he needed cargo space, so removing the bed wasn't an option. Lifting it would be expensive and impractical due to the independent front suspension. So Lee started looking for an SUV that would suit his needs, and considered getting a Toyota 4Runner or Isuzu Trooper. What he found appealing about the Cherokee was that not only did it have solid axles, but it had an engine and transmission that were tried and true. Lee turned to the Internet for more information and saw pictures of what could be done

Jeep XJ Profile: Lee Harper's 2001 XJ CONTINUED

Ancient rock art sites are one of the things Lee and his wife like to search for. Scientists think that the Indian petroglyphs shown here are between 5,000 and 10,000 years old.

The Maggiolina rooftop tent mounts to a Thule roof rack with three crossbars. It expands out with a hand crank in about a minute. This definitely beats pitching a tent!

with the Cherokee and he knew it was the right vehicle for the job.

Next came the search for the right Cherokee. Lee wanted an XJ that was as new as possible. He eventually found a 2001 XJ that was fully loaded with the Up Country suspension, tow package, and Selec-Trac 4WD. And the best thing? It was in cherry condition with only 9,000 miles! A month or so after the purchase, Lee paid me a visit to discuss his build-up. I almost died with envy when he opened the door revealing that it still had that "new car" smell!

After amassing all the parts he would need for the build-up, Lee was ready for action in a matter of a few short weeks. Lee chose the Rubicon Express 5.5-inch lift and upgraded it with adjustable control arms and JKS disconnects. Lee later found that with all the weight he would carry, which sometimes included 25 gallons of water along with food and supplies to last a few weeks, the rear leaf springs began to sag. A super heavy-duty AAL was added to compensate for the weight. This made the rear suspension even stiffer than before, but that was a necessary trade-off for this XJ's purpose.

For the 242 transfer case, Lee went with the Tom Woods SYE, but he had problems with the seal leaking. After search-

Lee's Jeep is an all-around well-built expedition vehicle. A Rubicon Express suspension and ARB locking differentials make it very capable off-road.

ing long and hard for a solution, Lee took the Jeep to MIT Garage of San Diego, where the SYE was rebuilt, eliminating the leaky seal.

The most recognizable feature on Lee's XJ is the rooftop tent. It is mounted to a Thule roof rack with three crossbars instead of two. Using a hand crank, the tent expands out in less than a minute. It has all the bedding inside with enough room to sleep two adults comfortably. The total weight of the tent is between 120 and 150 pounds. Lee's tent is the Maggiolina model, which is manufactured by Zifer of Italy and distributed by AutoHomeUSA.

Other modifications include a QuickAir2 air compressor for the ARB lockers and BushWacker flares that fully cover the tires and protect the sides of the Jeep from flying debris. The 33-inch MT/Rs are on 15 x 8–inch wheels with 4.5 inches of backspacing. Lee prefers the wheels tucked in and doesn't mind a little rubbing on the lower control arms. The Jeep is well armored with a Skid Row transfer-case skid, front and rear differential guards, the stock gas tank skid, and Rocky Road Outfitters step rails.

In between Lee's trips, I enjoy listening to his tales of bribing the Mexican police and the hazards of "tope," the Mexican speed bumps, or turning over rocks in the desert and finding rattlesnakes! I recently asked Lee how the XJ is working for him. His reply: "That Jeep will take me places I'm too scared to go." By the time this book is printed, Lee will have gone on his next expedition. He plans to drive to the Yucatan Peninsula to see the Mayan ruins and explore the jungles of Belize. Lee and his Jeep go on adventures that many people only dream about! ∎

The tent has plenty of room to sleep two adults comfortably. The only challenge is that sometimes it's hard to find a level spot to park when out on the trail.

WHEEL AND TIRE SELECTION

Off-road use can be hard on your wheels. This wheel received a lot of "rock rash" from a rocky section it just went through.

Virtually any type of wheel (steel, alloy, or aluminum) can be suitable for off-road use. However, while most people choose wheels based solely on appearance, there are some other factors you may want to consider. Alloy wheels are stronger than steel wheels, which can bend if hit hard enough against a rock. A bent wheel can sometimes be hammered back into shape, but often the wheel needs to be replaced. The fact that most steel wheels are considerably cheaper than alloys may offset that risk. Also, because steel wheels are inexpensive, it may be easier to stomach the scrapes and gouges that inevitably occur with serious off-road use, especially rock crawling.

Beadlocks

Beadlock wheels are the ultimate wheels for rock crawling. A beadlock wheel prevents the tire's bead from unseating from the rim when you're running at very low tire pressures. The bead of the tire is clamped between an outer ring and the rim of

This shows a typical beadlock wheel. The bead of the tire is held in place tightly by the outer ring, which is bolted to the wheel.

These are fake beadlocks. Cragar calls them Streetlocks, but they don't lock the bead in any way. The bolts around the wheel are just there to give it the beadlock look.

the wheel and locked in place when the bolts of the outer rim are properly torqued.

Although the benefits of beadlocks cannot be outweighed for rock crawling, there are several reasons some people prefer not to use them on a daily-driven rig. Aside from increased maintenance (like cleaning out the debris that collects inside the outer rim and checking the torque on the bolts), most beadlocks are not DOT-approved. But just because a wheel is not DOT-approved doesn't necessarily mean it's illegal in your state or that it will draw the attention of the authorities. After all, look at all the other modifications we do to our vehicles, very few of which are DOT-approved! However, this may be a concern if you live in a state that does strict inspections for registration. If you rarely, if ever, drive in terrain where beadlock wheels would be a benefit, but still want the beadlock look, fake beadlocks are available.

Wheel Size

Fifteen-inch wheels are the most commonly used size and the smaller diameter is useful for putting more rubber between the wheel and the terrain. The 16-inch wheels, which are more expensive, usually require metric tires with sizes displayed as 305/70R16, for example. These tires are also more expensive than the more common 33 x 12.50–inch tire (its equivalent on a 15-inch rim).

To calculate the size of a metric tire in inches, let's use the common stock size 225/75R15 as an example. The first number (225) is the width of the tire measured at the sidewalls in millimeters. Convert that to inches by dividing it by 25.4:

$$225 \text{ mm} \div 25.4 = 8.86 \text{ inches}$$
(tire width)

The second number of the metric tire size (75) is the aspect ratio, which is the height of the sidewall displayed as a percentage of the width. In this case, the sidewall height is 75 percent of the width. So,

$$8.86 \text{ inches} \times .75 = 6.645 \text{ inches}$$
(sidewall height)

Because there are two sidewalls, one above the wheel and one below it, multiply that number by 2 and add the diameter of the wheel, which is the third number in the size (15). This gives the actual diameter of the metric 225/75R15 tire in inches:

$$6.645 \text{ inches} \times 2 + 15 \text{ inches} = 28.29\text{-}$$
inch outside diameter

Along with considering the diameter of the wheel, you don't want to select a wheel that is too wide for your tires. Ideally, you want the tire's sidewall rubbing against rocks, not the rim, right? A wheel with a smaller width also helps keep the bead seated on the rim, which is always a good thing! I suggest the following wheel widths:

Wheel and Tire Width	
Wheel Width (inches)	Tire Width (inches)
7	9.50–10.50
8	10.50–12.50
9	11.50–13.50
10	13.50 +

These figures are just suggestions, and you may find that they differ slightly from what the tire manufacturer recommends. For example, Goodyear states that the approved rim width for 12.50-inch-wide MT/ Rs is 8.5 to 11.0 inches. Even though an 8-inch wheel is not technically "approved," tire manufacturer recommendations are very conservative and the 8-inch-wide wheel may be safe to use. But going with too wide a tire on a small wheel, such as a 12.50-inch-wide tire on a 7-inch wheel, results in the tire crowning, or bulging out, in the center of the tread, causing uneven wear.

Backspacing and Offset

Backspacing and offset are wheel measurements that determine how far the wheels (and tires) stick out. Backspacing is the distance from the

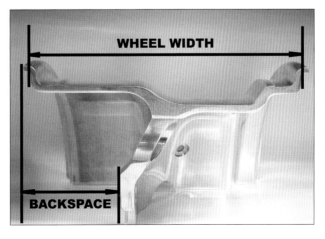

Backspacing is the distance from the inner mounting surface of the wheel to the edge of the rim. This distance determines how far the wheel will stick out. Stock XJ wheels have 5.25 inches of backspacing. (Photo Courtesy Tony Huntimer)

Choosing the proper backspacing is critical for lifted Jeeps with big tires. The taller the Jeep sits, the wider the track should be to keep it stable. More fender trimming may be necessary with tires and wheels that stick out farther.

inner mounting surface of the wheel to the inboard edge of the rim. Offset is the distance between the centerline of the wheel and the mounting surface. Backspacing is more common and easier to use when making wheel comparisons, so that is what I use throughout the book.

The more backspacing there is, the narrower the track. With less backspacing, the track is wider (the wheels stick out farther). Most stock XJ wheels have a backspace of 5.25 inches. By comparison, wheels with 3.75-inch backspacing stick out 1.5 inches farther on each side of the vehicle. Common aftermarket wheels have backspacing ranging from 4.75 to 3.25 inches.

Increasing the track using wheels with less backspacing is very important on a lifted Jeep for a number of reasons. Lifting a Jeep raises its center of gravity, which may increase the risk of a rollover both on- and off-road. Increasing the track gives it a wider stance and improves the stability of the Jeep in off-camber situations.

Choosing proper backspacing also helps prevent the tires from rubbing on the control arms and inner fenderwells. However, the farther the tires are spaced out, the more they rub on the fender and flares, so increased fender trimming may be needed. Keep in mind that some states are picky about how much tire can stick out past the flares. If this is the case for you, I recommend moving to another state, but if that's not possible, wider aftermarket flares such as BushWacker flares may become a necessity. The chart lists some recommendations on how much backspacing to run.

Wheel Spacers

Wheel spacers are another way to increase your track width. Avoid using cheap wheel spacers that simply slip over the stock lugs and are sandwiched between the wheel and hub. Use only spacers that bolt onto the lugs and have their own lugs for

These 1-inch wheel spacers are CNC-machined 6061 T6-grade aluminum.

Backspacing Guidelines			
Tire Size	**Lift Height (inches)**	**Fender Trimming**	**Recommended Backspacing (inches)**
235/75R15	Stock	None	Stock (5.25)
30 x 9.50	2	None	Stock
31 x 10.50	3	Minimal	Stock to 4.50
32 x 11.50	4.5	Yes	4.75 to 3.75
33 x 12.50	4.5 to 6	Yes	4.50 to 3.75
35 x 12.50	6	Aggressive	3.75 or less
37 x 12.50	6 to 8	Aggressive	3.75 or less Full-width axle swap

Dustin Mills owns this XJ with a 6.5-inch lift and 35-inch tires. This is an appropriate amount of lift for this tire size, but a good amount of fender trimming is needed to keep the tires from rubbing when the suspension flexes. Planning out how much lift and what tire size you want is a step in the right direction.

Tom Moser still had 31-inch tires on for this trip, but even with 4+ inches of lift and fender trimming, you can see how stuffed the front tires are in the fender. If he hadn't trimmed the fenders, he would have been pretty miserable with all the rubbing. In general, the more the tires stick out, the more you'll need to trim, and that includes guys running 31s.

the wheel. These wheel spacers can be costly, but you shouldn't sacrifice safety to save a few dollars. In some cases, it may be cheaper to just buy new wheels with less backspacing. If you are partial to a certain wheel, such as the popular Canyon wheels that came stock on some TJ Wranglers with 5.5-inch backspacing, using wheel spacers may be your only option. Wheel spacers can also be bought as "wheel adapters" to change bolt patterns. For instance, wheel adapters can allow you to use a 5-on-5.5-inch bolt pattern wheel with your stock 5-on-4.5-inch bolt pattern lugs.

Tire Size versus Lift Height

One of the most commonly asked questions is "How big a tire can I fit on X amount of lift?" Well, you could ask five people that question and get five different answers. That's because everyone's opinion on what "fits" differs by the way the XJ is driven and individual likes and dislikes. Does the Jeep need a lot of room to flex? Or does it only need enough flex to get over the speed bumps at the mall? Are you willing to trim the fenders, or are you okay with rubbing and sheet metal digging into your tires? Those are some of the questions that need to be answered before you can ask what size tires will work for you. To get you started, see the chart on page 46. It lists the most common lift and tire size combinations, as well as my recommendations on what wheel backspacing I think works best. Obviously, these are just suggestions based on my opinion for a capable XJ that flexes. In some cases, you could fit even larger tires than I've listed, if you are willing to trim more.

Correcting the Speedometer

When you upgrade to larger tires and/or different axle gears, your speedometer is no longer correct. Luckily, recalibrating the speedometer is cheap and easy to do on 1987–2001 XJs with an electronic speedometer. The process involves first knowing what size (number of gear teeth) speedometer gear you need, and then changing the speedometer gear located in the tail-shaft housing of the transfer case.

The quick and easy way to determine which gear you need would be to refer to a chart that tells you if you have X size tires, and X axle gear ratio, you need a speedometer gear with X number of teeth. Unfortunately, every chart I have come across has inaccurate recommendations. One reason for this is that the listed tire size can differ greatly from manufacturer to manufacturer. For example, a 33-inch BFG Mud Terrain has an actual tire diameter of only 32.8 inches, while a 33-inch Interco Super Swamper has an actual diameter of 33.7 inches. Both are listed as 33-inch tires, so would the same speedometer gear be correct for both tires? Certainly not! The following formula allows you to calculate exactly the number of teeth needed in your new speedometer gear.

Formula 1

New Tooth Count = (old tire diameter ÷ new tire diameter) x (new gear ratio ÷ old gear ratio) x old tooth count

If you don't know your old tooth count, and don't want to pull the gear to find out how many teeth it has, you can use the following formula. You can also use both formulas to double-check your calculations.

Speedometer gears come in various sizes and tooth counts. These small plastic gears can be purchased from a Jeep dealership for a little over $20 each, but you'll need to know which gear you need in advance. Don't forget to pick up a new O-ring while you're there.

This formula is provided courtesy of Mark Tener.

Formula 2

Number of Teeth in Speedo Gears = [63,360 ÷ (MSOD x 3.14159) x Axle Ratio] ÷ 74.5

where:

MSOD = Manufacturer's Stated Overall Diameter, the actual diameter of the tire

The answer is most likely a fraction, in which case you round up or down to the nearest whole number. Using my most recent tire purchase for *Project Rubicon* as an example, my 35-inch TrXus Mud Terrains have an actual diameter of 34.9 inches. Using Formula 1, I chose to use the factory speedo gear in my Jeep (34 teeth) and factory tire size (225/75R15 = 28.29 inches) to make sure my calculations are accurate. Back then, I also had stock 3.55:1 gears but have since re-geared to 4.56:1. Those numbers are needed as well. The calculation is as follows:

(28.29 inches ÷ 34.9 inches) x (4.56 ÷ 3.55) x (34) = 35.4 teeth

This tells me I need a speedometer gear with 35.4 teeth.

Using Formula 2, I get an answer of 35.37 teeth, which is close enough for our purposes (we're talking a difference of 3/100ths of a gear tooth).

With 35.4 teeth needed, I could choose either a 35- or 36-tooth

Speedometer Accuracy		
Speedometer Reading	Actual Speed per GPS	Speedometer Error
30 mph	30.6 mph	0.6 mph
40 mph	41.8 mph	1.8 mph
50 mph	52.4 mph	2.4 mph
60 mph	63.6 mph	3.6 mph
70 mph	74.5 mph	4.5 mph

speedo gear depending on whether I want the speedometer to read a little fast or a little slow. By the way, don't be concerned if it's off a little bit; rarely is any vehicle's speedometer 100 percent accurate. I chose to use the 36-tooth speedo gear so that as my tires wear, the speedometer reads more accurately as the tire's diameter gradually becomes smaller.

I wanted to further verify these calculations and my speed by using GPS. Before changing my speedo gear for the new tires, I had a 38-tooth gear, which matched my old 33s. I knew my speedometer was off with the 35s, so I built the chart (on page 48) using GPS; you can see how the difference is amplified at higher speeds.

After switching to a 36-tooth gear, I again tested my speedometer with GPS and found that it had an error of less than 1 mph at any of the speeds listed. The GPS unit that I used for this test was a newly purchased Magellan eXplorist 200.

Changing the Speedometer Gear 1987–2001

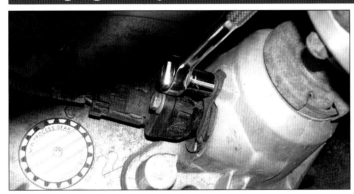

1 Locate the speedometer gear housing on the back of the transfer case. Remove the bolt holding the retaining clip.

2 Pull the speedometer gear housing from the transfer case. The speedometer gear will come out with it. Make sure that the rubber O-ring also comes out and isn't stuck inside the transfer case. It should still be attached to the plastic gear housing.

3 Even if the O-ring looks like it's in good condition, replace it with a new one. I have tried to reuse them, but the O-ring stretches out, which makes it difficult for the housing to fit back in and seat properly. You may also want to lubricate the O-ring with a little automatic transmission fluid so that it slides in more easily.

4 Replace the old gear with the new one. Make sure it snaps into place when you insert it into the plastic housing. The numbers in view on the plastic housing should correspond to the number of teeth on the gear (if not, the speedometer won't work). Rotate the gear housing so that the appropriate range is visible somewhere between the four and six o'clock position.

5 Replace the retaining clip, making sure it seats into the grooves in the gear housing. Snug the bolt, but do not over-tighten; it only requires 90 to 110 inch-lbs of torque.

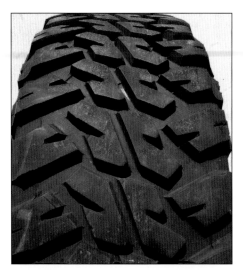

Goodyear MT/Rs are a very popular tire with an aggressive tread pattern. They are great in the rocks and snow, but not that great in the mud. MT/R stands for "Maximum Traction/Reinforced" (sidewall), not "Mud-Terrain." I have found these tires to be very friendly on the street as well.

The new Goodyear MT/R includes a Kevlar ply to the sidewall and an asymmetric (not directional) tread pattern. This new tread pattern offers improved on-road handling due to the tight center lugs and is better in the mud and rocks thanks to widely spaced outer lugs.

These BFGoodrich All-Terrains are a good trail tire. The voids between the lugs are not as wide as on mud-terrains so they won't fare well in the mud, but the numerous edges of the tread and siping make them great for wet pavement and icy roads.

Tread Types

The type of tread on your tires has a huge effect on off-road performance. If you like mud bogging, a good mud-terrain with an aggressive tread pattern is what you want. Mud tires are designed to self-clean, or throw the mud off the tire, not allowing the tread to become packed with it. The aggressive lugs on mud terrains along with strong sidewalls and good sidewall tread also make for good rock-crawling tires. The downside to having extremely aggressive tread is noise and handling on the street. Some people don't mind the constant "hum" of the tires on the pavement, but others hate it, especially as it gets louder once the tires start to wear. Of course, what is considered loud to one person might be quiet to another.

A typical all-terrain tire is much more pavement friendly and suitable for off-road, only it doesn't perform

So far I like my TrXus M/Ts by Interco, apart from the fact that they took a lot of weight to balance. The off-road traction is great and they do very well when aired down. The sidewalls do seem a little soft compared to the MT/Rs I had previously. Interco also added more siping, so even though it is a mud-terrain tire, it should do well for winter commutes.

nearly as well as an aggressive tread pattern. However, all-terrain tires are better for driving on ice and wet roads due to the increased number of edges in the tread biting at the road surface.

Siping (the little cuts or grooves) in the tread helps add more edges for more traction, and some companies are adding siping to their mud terrains for better on-road handling in

This is an IROK Super Swamper from Interco. The huge voids between the lugs make this an excellent tire for rocks and mud. (Photo Courtesy John Laurella)

This is ProComp's X-Terrain tire, which has a directional tread. The aggressive tread pattern is somewhere between a mud-terrain and all-terrain tire, so it's good for all-around use.

wet conditions. Siping can also be added to any tire by a tire shop.

Most off-road tires do well in a variety of terrain, but it would be best to select tires according to the terrain you encounter the most. If you do lots of mud, all-terrain tires are a no-no. On the other hand, all-terrains are usually better in deep sand where an aggressive tire digs too much. Sidewall strength should also be a concern if you like to play in the rocks.

The type of material used to make the tire, or its compound, also plays a part in how it handles and wears over time. In addition to the rubber, which contains many mineral and synthetic compounds by itself, the tire carcass is made of several plies of material including steel belts, polyester, nylon, and even Kevlar. Some tire manufacturers make bias-ply tires, but most tires are radials. The difference is the direction the cords of the plies run in the casing of the tire. The cords of a radial tire casing run at a 90-degree angle to the centerline of the tread. Bias-plies have cords that run only at an angle. This affects the way the sidewalls and tread conform to the road. Radial tires maintain a flat-

ter, more even contact patch, which is why they last much longer than bias-ply tires. Bias-ply tires tend to be cheaper than radials, so if your Jeep is a trail-rig only, bias-ply tires might be okay. Otherwise, for a Jeep that sees more pavement use, you get more life and a better ride using radials.

Some tires are directional, meaning they have tread that is meant to be used in a certain direction; they can only be used on one side of the vehicle and not rotated to the other

side. There are no problems using a directional tire unless you have a directional spare tire and need to use it on the wrong side of the vehicle. I prefer to do a five-tire rotation so that my spare is the same size and condition as the other tires. It also helps the tread last longer as a set, because each tire gets a chance to take a break when it's rotated to the spare position. For that reason, I prefer non-directional tires that can be put on any corner.

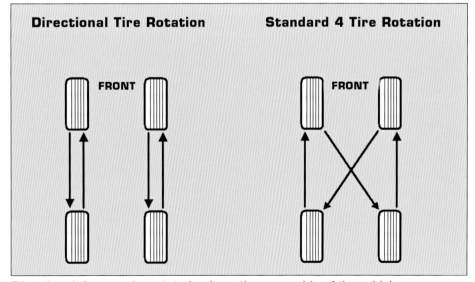

Directional tires can be rotated only on the same side of the vehicle. Non-directional tires can be used on either side of the vehicle.

Jeep XJ Profile: Bryan Vetrano's 1995 XJ

Bryan's 1995 XJ really stands out with his custom pillar-mounted lights, clear side-marker lenses, auxiliary lights, and the black-and-white color scheme.

Year: 1995
Engine: 4.0L I-6
Transmission: AW 4-speed
Transfer Case: NP231
Front Axle: Dana 30
Rear Axle: Chrysler 8.25
Gears: 3.55:1
Lockers: None yet
Steering: ZJ tie-rod
Suspension: 5-inch (Rusty's 3-inch + spacers)
Shocks: Rusty's
Tires: 33 x 12.50–inch Dayton Timberline MT
Wheels: 15 x 8 inches

Bryan purchased his 1995 Cherokee in 2000 and soon after installed its first lift: Rusty's 3-inch kit. After running that for a few years, Byran increased the lift to 5 inches to run 33s. In the front, he added a 1.75-inch coil spacer. For the rear, he added another stock shackle to each side, making a contraption similar to the TeraFlex revolver shackles. This increased the rear leafs' droop when flexing, but it didn't work well when the Jeep was loaded down because the shackles kept smacking against the frame. Bryan ended up ditching that setup and decided to rebuild the Rusty's 3-inch leaf pack by removing one of the Rusty's leafs and adding two leafs from an MJ Comanche. The end result was a six-leaf pack that Bryan says rides great and gave him the height he wanted. He also took the rear fender flares from the MJ, cut them to make two-piece flares, and attached them higher than the stock location. This meant attaching one piece to the passenger door and the other piece to the body. The MJ flare also matches his stock XJ front flare, which has also been raised to make way for fender trimming. The job was so well done that it looked like it came that way from the factory. The 33-inch tires on black 15 x 8–inch wheels with 4.75-inch backspacing are a good fit for this Jeep and they don't stick out too far.

As most Jeep owners know, a project Jeep is never finished, and Bryan continues adding unique modifications to his rig. The Jeep features two pillar lights on custom mounts. The rear bumper and tire carrier is also custom-made by Bryan. The beefy bumper has mounts that attach to the frame rails. It includes an integrated receiver, tow loops, and a mount for his Hi-Lift jack on the carrier. Rusty's metal taillight housings also give the rear of the XJ a little bit of style. Recovery and protection is handled by Rusty's tow hook brackets, Rusty's front and rear differential guards, and the Mopar (OEM) gas tank skid. Bryan cut out his rockers and welded in 2 x 4–inch steel for rock rails. His steering was upgraded with a ZJ tie-rod that is flipped above the knuckle using the Goferit Offroad tie-rod flip insert.

The interior of Bryan's XJ has plenty of modifications as well. He picked up an overhead console from the junkyard that, among other things, is a good place to hold his CB. He's also using X-Bound seat covers that fit pretty well considering they weren't made specifically for just the Cherokee. Toggle switches on the dash operate the pillar lights and auxiliary lights mounted on the front bumper. The Indiglo white-faced gauges in the instrument panel are another nice touch.

The transmission is cooled by an aftermarket cooler, and LeBaron hood vents have been added to the hood. Under the hood, Bryan is doing something unique. He cut a hole into the

Bryan fabricated his own beefy rear bumper and tire carrier. It includes shackle tabs and an integrated receiver. The metal taillight housings are from Rusty's Off-Road Products.

The dash features white-faced Indiglo gauges and toggle switches for the lights on the pillars and front bumper.

Jeep XJ Profile: Bryan Vetrano's 1995 XJ CONTINUED

firewall to relocate his K&N cone filter to the inside of the passenger-side cowl. This gives the engine colder air and protects the filter from water. When I met with Bryan to photograph his XJ, he had just completed this modification and still had to design a cover to protect the filter from water entering the top of the cowl. Removing the stock air box and routing the air tube into the firewall opened up lots of room in the engine compartment. Bryan plans on relocating the battery to where the stock air box was to make way for a belt-driven York air compressor.

Bryan plans to fabricate his own brackets to mount the York, and he's going to weld a V-belt pulley to the alternator pulley, similar to the brackets and pulleys offered by Kilby Enterprises at onboardair.com. A 2-gallon air tank will be mounted inside the Jeep for running the ARB lockers and airing up tires. I'm looking forward to seeing his onboard air system when it's completed!

In the near future, Bryan will also be installing a slip yoke eliminator and swapping in an XJ Dana 44 rear axle. Then both front and rear axles will get 4.88:1 gears and ARB lockers. A custom front winch bumper is in the works to match the heavy-duty custom rear bumper. ■

The 5 inches of lift is just right for the 33-inch tires, giving it an aggressive stance. With trimmed fenders and relocated flares, the 33s have plenty of room to flex.

Bryan routed his cone filter intake through the firewall and into the passenger-side cowl. The cold air makes more horsepower, and the filter stays dry.

STEERING, ALIGNMENT AND BRAKES

The stock steering is weak and can fail under the stress of big tires and certain off-road situations. At a minimum, carry a spare tie-rod. A better option is to upgrade the stock steering with a beefier unit.

The steering and brake systems are often forgotten in the early stages of most build-ups. But if "going big" is your plan, you want to consider some upgrades that will keep your Jeep safe on the street and help it perform better on the trail. Most people throw on the big lift and tires only to realize later that the stock steering and brakes are woefully inadequate.

Heavy-Duty Stock Steering Replacements

The stock steering is made up of a drag link from the pitman arm to the passenger-side knuckle and a tie-rod that connects the driver-side knuckle with the drag link. Although the stock steering can be used up to about 7.5 inches of lift, doing so

isn't recommended, as the joints start binding when the suspension is flexed. Not only does this limit the suspension travel, but it can also cause increased stress to the steering parts that may lead to breakage. If you're building an XJ with a lift in the 6-inch range or taller, you need to consider some steering upgrades due to this binding issue. Strength

This drag link is at such a steep angle that it is close to binding even though this XJ is on level ground. It has 7.5 inches of lift, and while this was drivable on the street, it would definitely bind when the suspension flexes off-road.

of the stock parts is also a concern. The tie-rod is made out of very weak thin-wall tube and will likely bend against the first rock it contacts. Like the tie-rod, the stock drag link is also very weak. A bent or broken steering part might ruin your day, especially if it leaves you stranded. For this

reason, steering upgrades are worth-while no matter how much, or how little, lift you have.

I feel that the best heavy-duty stock-replacement (that retains the stock geometry) steering is the Cur-rie HD steering system. Because it is a stock replacement, it's meant to

be an easy bolt-on, but I had to do some grinding on my extended sway bar mounts for clearance. (I proba-bly welded the extended mounts far-ther forward than stock.) The Currie drag link and tie-rod are 1.25-inch chrome-moly steel that is solid, not a hollow tube as is the stock stuff. The Currie tie-rod ends are massive com-pared to stock. Another benefit to the Currie system is that the ends of the drag link are angled to alleviate binding on lifted Jeeps. The angles are set to work best with 4 inches of lift, but per the Currie instructions, it can be used for Jeeps with 2 to 6 inches of lift.

One problem was encountered with the grease fittings. Some of them wouldn't take grease unless the joint was rotated into a certain position, and a couple wouldn't take grease at all. According to Currie, the ends come pre-greased and after a few thousand miles the joints should loosen enough to accept grease. If you have the Currie system with ends that don't take grease, do not try to force grease into them. A friend tried to grease them with a pneumatic

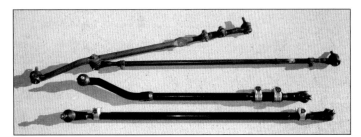

Currie Enterprises makes a heavy-duty stock replacement steering system designed for XJs with 2 to 6 inches of lift. While those are the recommendations from Currie, taller XJs can benefit from this steering upgrade, too.

This photo shows the Currie tie rod-and tie-rod end (bottom) compared to stock (top). Currie makes its own tie-rod ends, and they are massive compared to stock. The tie-rod itself is 1¼-inch thick solid steel, compared to the stock tie-rod, which is a hollow tube of about half the size.

The Currie drag link (bottom) is stronger than stock (top) and offers improved angles at the joints. This makes it less likely to bind on a lifted XJ.

This XJ has a ZJ tie-rod. ZJ tie-rods are stronger than stock XJ tie-rods, making them a good upgrade. The downside is that they come with a downward bend in them that gives up a little bit of clearance.

grease gun and actually blew out the back of one of the ends.

Another relatively cheap and easy steering upgrade is to replace the stock XJ tie-rod with a tie-rod from a ZJ Grand Cherokee with a V-8 engine. The ZJ tie-rod is a solid bar, which makes it much stronger.

The ZJ tie-rod ends are also slightly larger than the stock XJ ends. The downside to the ZJ tie-rod is that it has a downward bend to it, which gives up a little ground clearance compared to the straight XJ tie-rod. Nonetheless, most people consider it a worthwhile, low-budget upgrade.

Over-the-Knuckle and Cross-Over Steering Systems

One complaint about the steering knuckles on the Dana 30 is that there is no easy or affordable way to do an over-the-knuckle conversion. Over-the-knuckle refers to mounting the tie-rod and drag-link ends on

This picture shows an over-the-knuckle steering on a Dana 44 axle with flat-top knuckles. (Photo Courtesy John Laurella)

TeraFlex makes a High Steer knuckle that replaces the stock outer knuckle on the passenger side of the Dana 30. This gives the option of over-the-knuckle steering, but even if the drag link is mounted from below (as shown in this photo), it is still higher than stock.

This is the complete TeraFlex High Steer system on a Jeep Unlimited. The same setup can be installed on an XJ since they both use the Dana 30 front axle.

This is the U-Turn cross-over system by Off Road Only. It's a complete bolt-on system that will work with the track bar in the stock location. Of course, the components are much beefier than stock. For example, the tie rod is made of 1.375-inch 4130 chrome-moly. (Photo Courtesy Jason West)

Here you can see the Currie HD steering system with the driver-side tie-rod end mounted below the knuckle in the stock location.

This shows the tie-rod "flipped" to the top of the driver-side knuckle. This was done using the tapered insert sold by Goferit Offroad, Inc. It's a cheap and easy way to do over-the-knuckle steering on the driver's side.

top of the steering knuckle instead of from below. This lessens the angle of the drag link and provides clearance under the tie-rod. Over-the-knuckle steering can be done easily on a Dana 44 front axle, which makes swapping out the Dana 30 for a 44 that much more appealing. But any high-steer system is beneficial.

Cross-over steering systems are also very good but don't usually have as much clearance as an over-the-knuckle system. Either way, a few companies offer over-the-knuckle, high-steer, or cross-over steering conversion kits. TeraFlex, Off Road Only, JCR Offroad, Iron Rock Offroad, Rugged Ridge, Rusty's Offroad, and others offer steering kits. But beware; they are not cheap and you may need to make other modifications for the steering to work properly. For instance, the drag link should be parallel to the track bar. When it is not, adverse handling, such as bumpsteer, can occur. Bumpsteer is when uneven road or a bump causes the wheels to steer in an unwanted direction without input from the driver. The axle end of the

Project Rubicon *has the same Currie HD steering system, but the tie-rod has been flipped using the Goferit Offroad tapered insert. You can see the increase in clearance gained by flipping the tie-rod over the knuckle.*

A pitman arm from a 1993–1998 Grand Cherokee (ZJ, bottom) can be used to reduce the angle of the drag link. It produces a 3/4-inch drop compared to an XJ pitman arm (top).

track bar may need to be relocated to the top of the axle to keep it parallel with the drag link. Some kits may provide a bracket for this purpose.

Okay, so I said there is no cheap way to do over-the-knuckle on a Dana 30. There is a way to come close with the stock drag link and tie-rod. Goferit Offroad sells a tapered insert that allows you to flip the driver-side tie-rod to the top of the knuckle. This simple modification (which requires drilling and welding) gives the stock tie-rod as much clearance as an over-the-knuckle setup and more clearance than some other aftermarket steering systems. You cannot flip the passenger side because the drag link is bent in a way that would not work when flipped upside down. But if you are still set on having true over-the-knuckle steering, you could use the TeraFlex High Steer knuckle for the passenger's side, and the Goferit tie-rod flip on the driver's side.

Drop Pitman Arms

One way to improve the steering angle of the drag link is by installing a dropped pitman arm. Keep in mind that a dropped pitman arm alters the steering geometry unless you raise the track bar to keep it level with the drag link. If the drag link and track bar are not parallel, bumpsteer may result. Raising the track bar to above the axle may require you to shorten it as well. A stock pitman arm from a ZJ is the equivalent of a 3/4-inch drop on an XJ. Reportedly, bumpsteer with a ZJ pitman arm is very minimal.

Skyjacker offers a 2.5-inch Extreme Drop pitman arm. You should definitely raise the track bar when using this much drop to avoid bumpsteer. Also be aware that the increased leverage is going to add more stress to the steering box, so reinforcing it as described in the following section is highly recommended.

This is a perfect example of a track bar that has been raised above the axle to match the angle of the drag link for excellent steering geometry. When the track bar does not match the angle of the drag link, bumpsteer will occur. (Photo Courtesy John Laurella)

This C-ROK steering box reinforcement plate is one way to strengthen the steering box mount. Because XJ frame rails are thin and prone to cracking, reinforcing the steering box is highly recommended for anyone with 33-inch or larger tires and for anyone who just wants to strengthen the area.

Steering Box Reinforcement

One of the known weaknesses of the XJ is the relatively thin metal used for the frame rails. Although the lighter weight of the unibody can be seen as a large overall benefit, it can also cause some specific problems. One of those problems is the area that supports the steering box. Driving in off-road terrain, especially with large tires, greatly increases stress to the steering components. The steering box acts as a fulcrum where that stress is concentrated. Over time, cracks may develop in the frame around the steering box bolts. Once a crack appears, it will only get worse until the steering box is eventually ripped from the frame rail. If you plan on running 33- or 35-inch tires, you can expect cracks to develop in this area (if you don't have some already).

So how do you strengthen this area? Well, first of all, if you have exist-

ing cracks, they need to be welded. Then you can add a plate to this section of the frame rail that supports the three steering box bolts. Many aftermarket bumpers have mounts that support the steering box bolts, as well as the bumper bolts, thereby killing two birds with one stone.

Another solution is to use a reinforcement kit specifically designed for this problem. The C-ROK reinforcement kit is a bolt-on setup, while the JKS Steering Brace System is welded on. Either of these great products can be used to strengthen not only the outer frame rail, but the inner frame rail as well, giving the steering box a solid foundation to mount to.

Steering-box braces are also popular ways to add support to the steering box. However, I believe that a reinforcement plate for the frame rail would be money better spent if you had to choose between the two. A brace is designed to simply hold the steering box in a fixed position and keep it from moving, but a reinforcement plate adds strength to the source of the problem, which is at the frame rails. If you would like to use a steering-box brace, I recommend using it in addition to a reinforcement plate, not as a substitute.

Steering braces like this one from Rusty's Offroad do help, but they don't compare to reinforcing the steering box mounts the way C-ROK or JKS systems do. These steering braces can often be difficult to install and the frame end of the brace sometimes doesn't line up as well as intended.

Alignment: Toe, Caster and Camber

Changes to the front suspension and steering can affect the alignment, which is critical to the way the vehicle performs. It is important to address the alignment anytime changes are made.

Toe

The toe setting is the distance between the leading ends of the front tires compared to the distance between the trailing ends of the front tires. This measurement determines how much the front tires point in or out. This setting not only affects how the vehicle handles, but also is a big factor in how the tires wear. The toe is adjusted by rotating the tie-rod, which changes the length between the tie-rod ends. The toe setting should be set within the factory specifications, which are between 0 and +0.45 degrees. You can check and set your toe yourself. If you have big tires, you'll be fine if you toe-in the front to 1/4 inch or less.

Caster

Caster is the forward or rearward tilt (from vertical) of the

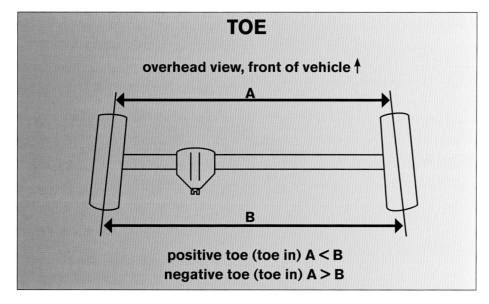

TOE

overhead view, front of vehicle ↑

A

B

positive toe (toe in) A < B
negative toe (toe in) A > B

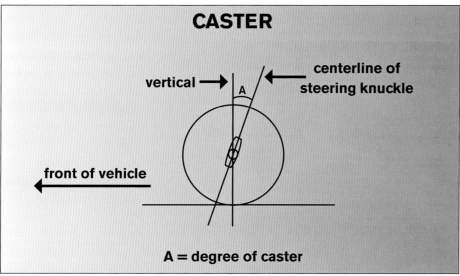

CASTER

vertical → A ← centerline of steering knuckle

front of vehicle

A = degree of caster

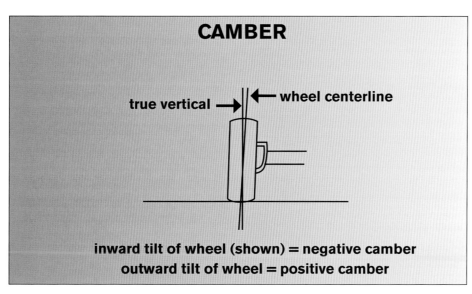

CAMBER

true vertical → ← wheel centerline

inward tilt of wheel (shown) = negative camber
outward tilt of wheel = positive camber

steering knuckle. The top of the knuckle should always be tilted to the rear, which results in a positive caster reading. Even on lifted XJs, you should try to keep the caster within the factory specifications, which are between +5.25 and +8.5 degrees, with a preferred setting of +7.0 degrees.

Caster can be adjusted with small shims placed between the lower control-arm frame mount and the inner sleeve that holds the control arm. If you have adjustable control arms, the caster can be adjusted more easily by changing the length of the arms. Be aware that changing the caster also changes the pinion angle of the front differential, which may result in front driveline vibrations. The pinion angle should take preference over the caster, so if you cannot get the caster within the recommended range without front driveline vibration, set the caster to the greatest amount possible before vibrations occur. It is not uncommon for lifted XJs to have poor caster, some even into the +3.0-degree range.

Camber

Camber is the inward or outward tilt of the wheel relative to the center of the vehicle. Pre-runner trucks often have a lot of camber that is noticeable with the tops of the tires angled into the body. On stock XJs, camber is not adjustable, so if your tires are angled in like a pre-runner truck, I'd say you've jumped the XJ one too many times and bent the axle! Factory specifications for camber are −0.75 to +0.5 degree, with −0.25 degree preferred. If you should need to adjust the camber, you have to do it with special adjustable ball joints. Bad camber is most commonly associated with a bent axle

You can do your own alignments if you are so inclined. The toe is not that difficult to do. These MT/Rs had a seam in the case of the tire that was uniform all the way around. That was a good place from which to measure.

The steering stabilizer's job is to dampen minor vibrations that occur in the steering. A bad steering stabilizer cannot be the cause of death wobble, and installing a new stabilizer is not a cure for death wobble; it only covers it up until the new stabilizer goes bad too.

housing and, if it is bad enough that it needs correction, it may be better to replace the whole axle rather than to try to correct it.

Death Wobble

The weather was very nice considering it was early November in northern Nevada. Our group of XJs, a TJ, and an Unlimited was making its way through a very rocky trail called Bronco Canyon, when Steve, driving a lifted and modified XJ, managed to bend his stock tie-rod into a nice "V" shape. He also bent his steering stabilizer so badly that it was not salvageable. After swapping in a spare tie-rod, we were back on our way. We didn't adjust his toe alignment; it looked good enough, so we knew it would work to get him home. His alternator was also going out, so I followed him back into town to make sure he'd get home safely. Going about 40 mph, every now and then (usually after hitting a bump in the road) Steve's front tires would start wobbling back and forth violently and wouldn't stop until he slowed to almost a complete stop. He also told me the steering wheel was jerking back and forth so badly that it was difficult to even maintain his grip. Following him from behind, I knew exactly what he had: the dreaded "death wobble"!

Death wobble, while more common on lifted XJs, can happen to stock Cherokees as well. The cause is bad alignment, unbalanced wheels, a loose or worn part, or a combination of all the above. The front axle has many moving parts that are spinning at a high rate, including the wheels, axle shafts, U-joints, and bearings, all of which resonate (or vibrate) at a certain frequency at high speeds. Add to that the steering and ball joints, which allow these spinning parts to rotate and spin on different planes, changing the resonance. Minor vibration is normal. That is why every stock XJ came with a steering stabilizer from the factory to dampen these minor vibrations. But when these vibrations get out of control, death wobble can occur.

One common misconception is that a worn steering stabilizer causes death wobble, or that a new steering stabilizer will cure it. Neither is true. If you replace the steering stabilizer hoping it will cure death wobble, it may mask the vibrations, but death wobble will rear its ugly head again because the problem still exists. With a well-maintained Jeep, it is possible to drive without a steering stabilizer at all and not have death wobble. That is a good test to see how healthy your XJ is.

Fixing death wobble means finding the cause, and that's not always an easy task. In Steve's case, I'm sure the condition of his wheels and tires had a lot to do with it. He was running 33-inch Super Swampers that had seen better days, and I don't think his wheels had been balanced recently, if ever! The fact that he had just changed tie-rods and his alignment was also suspect didn't help. To find the cause of death wobble, you need to troubleshoot each potential problem starting with the easiest and least expensive. It's a process of elimination. Here are some suggestions of what to check:

- Rotate the tires and make sure each tire has even air pressure.
- Have the wheels and tires balanced.
- Check the track bar bolts for tightness and the bushings for wear; replace as needed.

- Get an alignment. Poor caster is a common contributor for death wobble.
- Check the ball joints; replace as needed.
- Check the tie-rod ends; replace as needed.
- Check the unit hubs; replace as needed.
- Check the control-arm bolts and bushings; replace as needed.

Rear Disc-Brake Conversion

You will definitely notice that it takes longer to stop with bigger tires. The stock brakes are marginal at best for a stock XJ, and much worse with bigger tires. This is partly because the bigger, heavier tire has more rotating mass, which makes it more difficult to stop. Part of the problem is that all XJs came with drum brakes in the rear. Some XJs have

10-inch drums, but *Project Rubicon* had even smaller 9-inch drums on its 8.25-inch Chrysler axle. It is a wonder that DaimlerChrysler never switched to rear disc brakes on the Cherokee, considering all the other modern improvements they made over the years. Even though DaimlerChrysler never did it, converting from drums to discs is the best brake system upgrade you could ever do.

When planning your disc-brake conversion, you have a couple of different alternatives. The most popular conversion is to swap disc brakes from a ZJ Grand Cherokee, which can be done cheaply with junkyard parts. It's a fairly straightforward swap. You have to widen the center hole of the backing plate if you have the Chrysler 8.25-inch or Dana 44 axle, and you may need some custom work to hook up the emergency-brake cables. The same conversion has also been

Rear disc brakes are probably the best brake upgrade you can do. Not only will rear discs give you more stopping power, but they are also much easier to work on than drum brakes.

This TeraFlex kit includes most of the same parts as the ZJ rear disc conversion. You need a new backing plate, rotors, calipers, brake pads, and flexible brake hoses.

made with disc brakes from a Ford Crown Victoria. A few companies make kits to make the conversion even easier.

The junkyards in my area would only sell the complete axles and would not separate the brake assemblies. For *Project Rubicon*, I also wanted to use all new parts, so I chose to install the kit made by TeraFlex. This kit can be used on the Dana 44, 8.25, or Dana 35 C-clip or non-clip axles. It uses Ford Explorer rotors drilled for 5-on-4.5-inch and 5-on-5.5-inch bolt

patterns. The backing plate is custom made by TeraFlex and includes an internal drum emergency brake. Installing this kit is very much the same as the ZJ swap, only you don't need to widen the center hole on the backing plate. This installation is slightly different if you have a non–C-clip axle.

Once I finished the install, the benefits of rear discs were immediately noticeable on the first test drive. Not only was the stopping distance reduced, it also took less pedal pressure to bring the Jeep to a stop. There is definitely a big improvement over the stock drums. This was a very worthwhile modification, and I recommend using rear disc brakes no matter what rear axle you have.

Installing Rear Disc Brakes

1 After blocking the front wheels, put the rear axle on jack stands and remove the rear wheels and drums. Remove the differential cover and drain the gear oil into a suitable catch pan.

2 *Remove the retaining pin that holds the cross shaft. The stock carrier used a retaining pin with a regular bolt head, but in this case, my ARB retaining pin requires a hex key.*

3 *You are then able to slide the cross shaft out of the differential. Then, rotate the carrier back to the position where the ends of the shafts and C-clips are visible.*

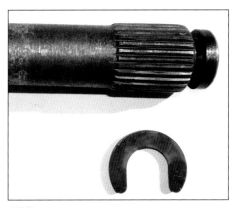

4 *Remove the axle shafts by pushing the shaft in toward the center of the axle to release the C-clips. They might fall out on their own, so make sure you retrieve them from inside the differential. Once the clips have fallen out, the shafts can be pulled out of the axle. Be careful not to damage the bearings when removing the shafts.*

5 *This is how the drum brake looks once the shafts have been removed. It is a good idea to stuff a clean rag in the tube opening to keep dirt out.*

6 *Disconnect the brake line and have something ready to collect the brake fluid that drains out.*

7 Remove the entire drum brake assembly and then unbolt the backing plate.

8 Once the backing plate is removed, this is all that's left. Now you're ready to begin the actual installation.

9 Before you install anything, bend the hard line into position. I bent mine straight up as the photo shows. You will understand why later in the install.

10 Install the backing plate. If you're using a ZJ backing plate, you'll need to bore out the center hole of the backing plate to get it to fit.

11 Now you're ready to reinstall the axle shafts. This was a good time for me to swap in my new alloy shafts, but the stock shafts also work fine.

12 Slide the rotor onto the axle shaft flange. Keep some brake cleaner handy to make sure any grease that gets on the rotors can be cleaned off.

13 Clip the brake pads into the calipers. There is a right- and left-side caliper and right- and left-side pads, so make sure they're all installed correctly.

14 Install the caliper onto the rotor. Tighten caliper bolts to spec.

15 *Install the flexible brake hose. The TeraFlex instructions said to weld the bracket to the axle tube. I just modified the bracket to attach to the leaf spring plate instead. I thought it was easier to bend the hard line to this position rather than have it lower at the axle tube.*

16 *If you didn't reinstall the C-clips, cross shaft, and retaining pin when you put the shaft back in, now is the time to do that. Don't forget to put the differential cover on and fill it with gear oil. Then you can bleed the brake system.*

17 *The kit doesn't include a way to connect the emergency-brake cable to the new emergency brake. After driving it around for two weeks with it disconnected, I wrapped the cable around the lever and put a clamp on it. The emergency brake isn't as tight as I would prefer, but it's good enough for now.*

18 *Once everything is back together you can put the wheels on and enjoy your new brakes. In case you were wondering, I didn't need to install a different proportioning valve or modify the master cylinder per the TeraFlex instructions. Your results may vary. With 15-inch wheels, you need wheels with 4.5 inches of backspacing or less to clear the caliper.*

Jeep XJ Profile: Garrett Bird's 1996 XJ, *The Bird-Mobile*

The front end of Garret's XJ has been beefed up substantially. It features a Rigidco front bumper, Currie HD steering, and Barnett HD differential cover.

Year: 1996
Engine: 4.0L I-6
Transmission: AX15 5-speed manual
Transfer Case: NP231 + AA, SYE + 4:1
Front Axle: Dana 30
Rear Axle: Dana 44
Gears: 4.88:1
Lockers: Detroit front and rear
Steering: Currie HD system
Suspension: 7.5-inch custom long-arm
Shocks: ProComp
Tires: 35 x 12.50–inch Goodyear MT/Rs
Wheels: 15 x 8–inch Cragar Street Locks

Garrett bought his XJ in late 2004 for the sole purpose of building it into a serious trail rig. With only about six months into the build-up, there is more to be done to this rig before it's finished (no Jeep is ever finished, right?), but Garrett has already invested a lot into the drivetrain and axles. The NP231 transfer case has been upgraded with the TeraFlex 4:1 low range and Advance Adapters HD slip yoke eliminator. With the 4:1 low range in the transfer case and 4.88s in the differentials, this XJ can really crawl!

The front axle is the stock Dana 30 beefed up with Superior shafts and the Currie HD steering system. The rear is a swapped-in XJ Dana 44. Detroit lockers in the front and rear keep all four 35-inch Goodyear MT/Rs turning.

The long-arm suspension is custom built by TeraFlex, featuring the company's own heavy-duty adjustable control arms with massive modular ends. TeraFlex coils and coil spacers lift the front and Skyjacker leafs with TeraFlex shackles lift the rear. This suspension gave 7.5 inches of lift

Jeep XJ Profile: Garrett Bird's 1996 XJ, *The Bird-Mobile* CONTINUED

Garrett tests the flex of the TeraFlex suspension. With 7.5 inches of initial lift and trimmed fenders, there is plenty of room to flex with 35-inch Goodyear MT/Rs.

The TeraFlex long-arm suspension features incredibly beefy lower control arms with huge modular joints.

initially, but it may come down a bit once all the rock rails and skid plates are added. The long-arm suspension offers good amounts of flex, limited only by the shock length, which is typical for most XJ suspensions.

Garrett has added a Rigidco front bumper that includes an integrated receiver and incredibly beefy tow loops. The bumper includes an excellent mounting system with brackets that plate both frame rails, adding support to the steering box. A steering-box brace adds even more support. The axles are protected by heavy-duty Barnett differential covers from T&J Performance.

Garrett's plans are to add some more protection in the form of rock rails and skid plates and maybe even a full exo-cage. ■

This rock-crawling section was a piece of cake with 4:1 low range in the transfer case, 4.88:1 in the differentials, and two Detroit lockers.

CHAPTER 5

AXLES, GEARING AND TRACTION DEVICES

Stock Front Axles

With the exception of the Dana 44 front axles used in the XJs exported to South America, all other XJs come with Dana 30 front axles. Not all Dana 30s are the same, however, and different versions were used in the Cherokee.

Vacuum-Disconnect Dana 30

Many XJs built between 1984 and 1991 have a vacuum-disconnect, high-pinion Dana 30 front axle. The additional housing that wraps around the passenger-side axle tube easily identifies this axle setup. Inside the housing, a shift fork engages the front axle when the transfer case lever is pulled into 4WD. The vacuum lines running from the transfer case to the front axle are prone to leaks due to age and normal wear and tear over the years. Trying to troubleshoot and repair a faulty vacuum-disconnect system can be a major headache. Some people have found ways to lock the shift lever in place by keeping the shafts engaged so that they always turn as on a non-disconnect axle. But it isn't that difficult to eliminate

The vacuum-disconnect axle is easily recognized by the additional housing around the passenger-side axle tube.

JEEP CHEROKEE PERFORMANCE UPGRADES 1984–2001   71

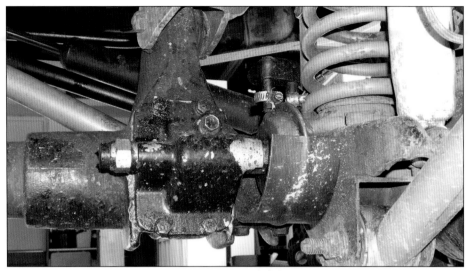

This view from behind the axle shows the shift-motor housing. Vacuum lines (not shown in this photo) from the transfer case connect to the shift motor and operate the shift fork.

Here is the shift motor removed from the axle. You can see the shift fork (on the right) that engages the shafts.

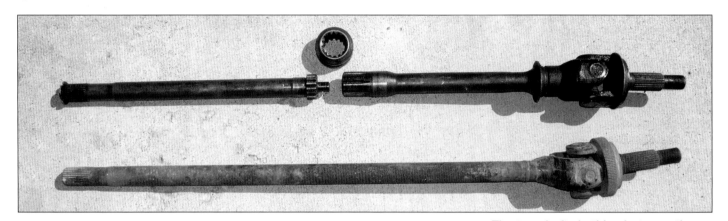

The top shafts in this photo are the disconnect shafts. Some of the inner shafts have C-clips and others do not. The two shafts are locked together by the small collar that is moved by the shift fork. The shaft on the bottom is a one-piece shaft from a non-disconnect axle. This shaft was badly rusted, so it was not used in the conversion.

Warn makes a block-off plate and includes the seals needed for the conversion to eliminate the vacuum-disconnect system. The only other thing needed is a passenger-side one-piece axle shaft.

With the shift motor removed, you can see the inner shaft still in the axle. This inner shaft was the C-clip version, so it was kind of a pain to get it out.

The new one-piece shaft is installed, successfully eliminating the two-piece shaft and vacuum disconnect. All that was left to do was install the Warn plate to seal the opening.

The non-disconnect front axle offers more reliable four-wheel-drive engagement. When the vehicle is in motion, the axle shafts are always turning, even when not under power. When the four-wheel-drive lever is pulled into one of the four-wheel-drive modes, power is sent to the wheels.

the whole vacuum-disconnect system, including the shift motor, and replace the passenger-side two-piece axle shaft with a non-disconnect axle shaft and new seals. These earlier versions of the Dana 30 came with small 5-260x U-joints, unless the XJ had ABS brakes, in which case it was upgraded to the larger 5-297x U-joints. Some very early XJs (1984 to 1985 or so) even had CV–jointed shafts, which are recognizable by the rubber boot covering the axle shaft at the joint.

Non-Disconnect High-Pinion Dana 30

All 1992–1999 XJ front axles are non-disconnect high-pinion Dana 30s. Some still had the smaller 5-260x U-joints, but 1995 and later XJs all have 5-297x U-joints. These non-disconnect axles with stock shafts and 5-297x (or replacement Spicer 5-760x) U-joints are not a bad axle, and they can hold up to 33-inch tires. Even 35-inch tires are possible, but alloy shafts and stronger U-joints are recommended. No matter what tire size you are running, it's a good idea to carry spare shafts. Most often it is the U-joint that breaks, and when that happens, it almost always destroys the ears of the axle shafts.

Low-Pinion Dana 30

The 2000 and 2001 XJs have a low-pinion Dana 30, which is identical to the Dana 30 used in the TJ (1997 and later) Wranglers. This is also a non-disconnect axle with the 5-297x U-joints. The shafts can be interchanged between the XJ high-pinion axles and vice versa. The low-pinion axle has three disadvantages: increased angle between the pinion and the driveshaft, less driveshaft clearance, and a slightly weaker

This is a 5-297x U-joint that broke on the trail. The XJ had 35-inch tires and a front locker. It was going in reverse on a very rocky trail with the wheel turned when it snapped. As you can see, the broken U-joint took out the ears of the shafts as well.

This is a low-pinion Dana 30 axle in a 2001 XJ. Notice how the pinion is below the centerline of the axle.

ring and pinion. The ring-and-pinion strength issue shouldn't be a concern unless you are running larger than 35-inch tires or are particularly hard on the axle. The real disadvantages are the pinion angle, which might cause driveline vibrations if you have a lot of lift, and the driveshaft being more exposed to potential hazards such as rocks. Many TJ owners choose to swap out their low-pinion Dana 30s in favor of the non-disconnect high-pinion XJ Dana 30.

Stock Rear Axles

Several different factory rear axles were used under the Cherokee. It is critical that you are able to identify which axle you have so you can decide if it is worth keeping, worth upgrading, or should be discarded for something better. The following sections describe the strengths and weaknesses of the factory axles and available upgrades that can increase their strength and reliability.

This is a high-pinion Dana 30. Its pinion is above the centerline of the axle. High-pinion axles are preferred because they offer more driveshaft clearance, better driveshaft angles, and are slightly stronger.

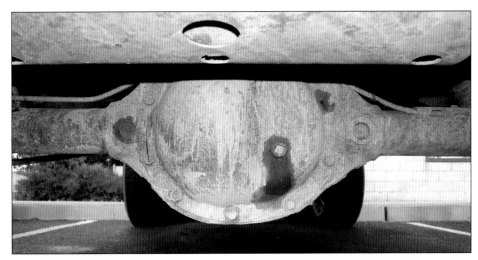

This is a Dana 35, identified by its oval cover and housing. It is the least desirable of all XJ rear axles due primarily to the weak housing and small axle tubes. It came in both C-clip and non–C-clip versions.

Dana 35

The first rear axles in the Cherokee were the non–C-clip Dana 35 axle used from 1984 to 1986. In 1987, Chrysler switched to a C-clip version of the same axle. You often see these axles listed as D35C, but the "C" does not stand for C-clip. It stands for "custom," as in the axles were shipped unfinished by the Dana Corporation. Although suitable for a stock XJ, these axles do not hold up well to large tires and lockers. The weakness of the Dana 35 is found in the small 27-spline shafts, small axle tubes, and a small ring gear. Although I have witnessed a few Dana 35s on the trail pushing around 35-inch tires, I think it's safe to say that it's not a question of "if" they break, but rather "when." Personally, I would not trust a Dana 35 above a 31-inch tire and an open differential. Also be wary of C-clip axles, because if you break a C-clipped axle on the trail, the wheel can fall off.

Several lockers are available for the Dana 35, but adding one increases the stress to an already weak axle. The best upgrade to a Dana 35 axle is . . . a different axle! But, I realize there are some cases where swapping axles isn't an option. If you decide to spend money on this axle, Superior and Yukon make Super 35 kits that include 30-spline axle shafts. That strengthens the shafts considerably, and adding a truss to the housing keeps it from bending. The overall strength of the axle is increased quite a bit; however, the ring gear is still only 7.5 inches, which is very small. These kits aren't cheap, so spending that much money on a Dana 35 is questionable.

Dana 44

The Dana 44 was only used in 1987–1989 XJs and appears to have been limited to some of those with the towing package. With 30-spline shafts and thick tubes, this is a great stock axle for 35-inch tires. You can go even bigger with alloy shafts. The weakest part of the Dana 44 is the pinion size, but this usually isn't a problem with the tire sizes run on XJs.

There is wide aftermarket support for the Dana 44, and the ability to gear down to 5.38:1 or even lower makes it a very sought-after "stock" axle. The fact that it doesn't have C-clips is also appealing.

The strongest rear axle available in the XJ was the Dana 44, but Chrysler put them only in some XJs for 1987–1989 with the optional towing package. The differential cover is not oval as is the Dana 35; it has more of an offset point at the bottom.

27-Spline Chrysler 8.25-Inch

Chrysler started using the 8.25-inch axle alongside the Dana 35 in 1991. It is a C-clip axle, and none were used on XJs with ABS brakes. The 27-spline shafts are comparable to the Dana 35, but they might even be slightly weaker because they neck down after the splines even more than the Dana 35s. However, the 3-inch-diameter axle tubes make up for it, bringing the overall strength equal to or slightly better than the Dana 35s.

One disadvantage of the 8.25 is that the differential housing has worse ground clearance than both the Dana 35 and Dana 44, largely due to the big lip on the bottom that likes to get hung up on rocks. Much of this lip can be ground down, or "shaved," to improve its clearance. As with the Dana 35, I wouldn't feel comfortable using anything larger than 31-inch tires with this 8.25, although some people do run larger and get away with it.

There isn't much aftermarket support for the 27-spline 8.25-inch axle. There are a few locker options, but similar to the Dana 35, many people feel it isn't worth the money to upgrade this axle. It is possible to convert it to use 29-spline shafts. You need a pair of 29-spline shafts from a newer 8.25, but you must also swap carriers or install a locker that

The Chrysler 8.25-inch housing has a flat bottom. The housing is strong but the 27-spline shafts are weak. The 1997-and-newer 8.25 has stronger 29-spline axles.

includes a carrier for a 29-spline 8.25. Depending on the cost of the shafts and carrier, you might be able to find a complete 29-spline axle and swap the whole thing out for about the same cost.

29-Spline Chrysler 8.25-Inch

The 29-spline Chrysler 8.25 was used in 1997 through 2001 XJs alongside the Dana 35. These C-clip 8.25 axles are very common in these newer XJs, but none were used in XJs with ABS brakes. All XJs with ABS were stuck with the Dana 35. Versions of this 29-spline axle are also used in the Dodge Durango and Dakota pickup, as well as the

Jeep Liberty. In my opinion, the 29-spline version of the Chrysler 8.25 is probably the most underestimated XJ axle because it's "stock" and "not a Dana 44," but it is a decent axle. With stock shafts, it can easily handle 33-inch tires, and can handle 35s with alloy shafts. Also, the right- and left-side shafts are equal lengths, so you only need to carry one shaft for a spare.

There is more aftermarket support for this axle than the 27-spline version. ARB, Detroit, PowerTrax, and Aussie Locker make popular lockers for this axle. With alloy shafts, these axles are extremely durable and handle plenty of abuse.

	Stock Axle Comparison				
	Spline Count	Shaft Diameter at Splines (inches)*	Shaft Diameter at Neck Down (inches)*	Tube Diameter (inches)	Ring Gear
Dana 44	30	1.281	1.234	2.75	8.50
29-Spline 8.25	29	1.250	1.141	3.00	8.25
Dana 35	27	1.172	1.117	2.62	7.58
27-Spline 8.25	27	1.148	1.039	3.00	8.25
* Measurements were taken with a vernier caliper and rounded off to the nearest 1/1,000 inch.					

This shows the difference between a C-clip shaft (bottom) and a non–C-clip shaft. The top is a Dana 44 axle, while the bottom is a 29-spline C-clip 8.25 shaft. The C-clip keeps the shaft in the housing. Non–C-clip shafts, such as the Dana 44, have a retainer plate that bolts to the outboard end of the axle housing.

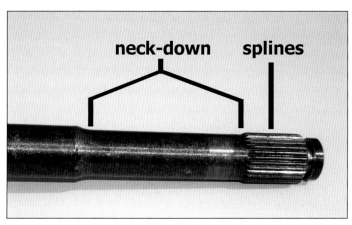

neck-down   splines

This is a profile of a Chrysler 8.25 shaft. All stock rear axle shafts neck down after the splines. Some shafts neck down more than others. This helps the shaft twist and not break. The Chrysler 8.25 shafts have much more neck-down compared to the Dana shafts, and I am unsure why that is.

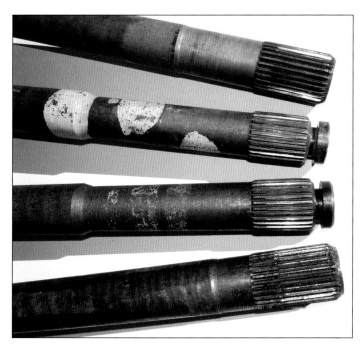

With the stock axle shafts side by side, can you tell which is which? From the top down, they are a non–C-clip Dana 35, a C-clip 27-spline 8.25, a C-clip 29-spline 8.25, and a Dana 44.

Alloy Axle Shafts

Upgrading to alloy axle shafts is a great way to add some strength, and you can save your stock shafts as spares.

Stock shafts are usually made from carbon-based 1040 steel, which the axle-shaft industry considers a soft steel. The introduction of other metals to the carbon steel can add strength, hardness, and the ability to return to their original shape after being twisted. Alloy shafts are also heat-treated, which adds even more strength and hardness.

Many rear axle shafts are made from 1541h steel that contains manganese. According to Yukon Gear & Axle, their 1541h shafts are 20 to 25 percent stronger than stock. Even harder is 4340 chrome-moly, which is up to 39 percent stronger than stock. You may notice that 1541h is reserved for most rear axle applications. Although 4340 chrome-moly has excellent twisting properties, it does not react to bending as well as 1541h. Because the rear axles are semi-floating, the shafts support some of the vehicle's weight, and must be able to bend without breaking. Technically, the front axles are also semi-floating, but do not carry

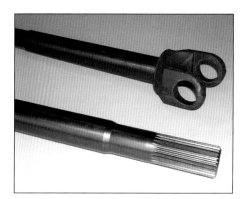

These Warn front shafts are made of 4340 chrome-moly and are through-hardened.

This Yukon rear shaft for the 8.25 is made from 1541h and is induction-hardened. Yukon shafts are an estimated 25 percent stronger than the stock shafts.

nearly as much of the load as the rear shafts.

Also important to shaft strength is the heating process; there are two common types: induction hardening and through hardening. Simply put, induction hardening hardens the surface of the shaft to a certain depth, leaving a softer core. Through hardening, as the name suggests, hardens the entire shaft all the way through. These processes help determine how well a shaft returns to its original shape after being twisted, which is key to shaft strength.

Another thing to consider when choosing a shaft is whether the splines are cut or rolled. Rolled splines are much stronger because no material is removed and the splines are formed before the shaft is heat-treated.

Popular Axle Swaps

Sometimes it just doesn't make sense to spend any money on upgrading a stock axle. When you need something stronger, it's time for an axle swap.

Front Axle Swaps

A few axles are a direct bolt-in swap for the Dana 30. Whether or not they are a worthwhile swap is debatable. One such axle is the Rubicon 44 out of a Rubicon TJ. This axle has a Dana 44 center section, but the tubes, ball joints, and steering knuckles are Dana 30, so it isn't much of an upgrade in terms of strength. In addition to that, it's low pinion, which isn't desirable at all. The only good thing it has going for it is the factory selectable locker that is included in all Rubicons.

If you have a 2000 or 2001 XJ with the low-pinion Dana 30, it can be replaced with a high-pinion 30 from an older XJ and it is a direct swap. The best ones to swap in come with non-disconnect axles (from 1990 on). Dana 30s before that have slightly different knuckles, so if you go that route, you need to keep your newer knuckles. The axle shafts from your 2000 or 2001 do work in the older housing as well. Also, if you want 4.10:1 gearing, pull one out of an XJ with the 2.5L 4-cylinder engine, as these came with 4.10s stock. If you do the swap from low pinion to high pinion, I recommend you have at least 3 inches of lift because the driveshaft has been known to contact the exhaust on the 2000 and 2001 models.

The only other bolt-in axles are custom-built from companies such as Currie Enterprises. They have Dana 44 axles that can bolt up to your XJ and

Here are a full-width Dana 44 (left) and a Ford 9-inch axle (right); they were pulled out of a 1975 Ford F-150. They are good candidates for a swap but will need quite a bit of fabrication and welding before they will fit under an XJ.

This is John Laurella's full-width Dana 44 that he swapped from a 1979 Ford. He used the Rubicon Express bracket kit and a custom track-bar mount. (Photo Courtesy John Laurella)

then stuff them with a variety of gear and locker options to suit your needs. This option isn't cheap, but the alternative is to do what most people do, which is find a Dana 44 from another vehicle and make it work using fabrication and welding.

One popular donor vehicle for a Dana 44 front axle is the 1980 and newer Wagoneer or Grand Wagoneer. The 61.5-inch WMS to WMS (wheel mounting surface) width of this axle is close to the stock XJ axle's 60.5-inch width. Aftermarket shafts are readily available for this axle. The Wagoneer has a leaf-sprung front suspension, so unless you plan to convert your front to leafs, you need to weld on new coil buckets and control-arm mounts. Bracket kits are available from Rubicon Express and others. The one major disadvantage to using a Wagoneer front axle is that it has a low pinion, but some consider this an acceptable tradeoff for the added strength. The Wagoneer Dana 44 uses a 6-on-5.5 bolt pattern, which is good if you are also swapping in a rear Wagoneer axle to match, or the bolt pattern can be converted to 5-on-5.5.

Other Dana 44 front axles can be found under F-100, F-150, or F-250 Ford trucks from the 1970s. Specifically, the F-100 and F-150s from 1970 to mid-1976 are high pinion and have a 5-on-5.5-inch bolt pattern. F-250 axles are 8-lug and only 1978–1979 are high pinion. Try to avoid later axles (1977–1979) as they have cast suspension mounts that are more of a challenge to remove when setting up your new brackets. Ford axles are full-width (about 67 inches WMS to WMS), high pinion,

and have the pumpkin on the driver's side. They are paired with either a Ford 9-inch or Dana 60 rear axle. Using wheels with more backspacing can narrow the track a little, if desired, or you can narrow the axle to accept Wagoneer shafts. Doing this correctly requires precise fabrication and welding skills.

Rear Axle Swaps

Because some stock axles are better than others, if you have the Dana 35 or 27-spline 8.25, you could swap in an XJ Dana 44 or 29-spline 8.25. Either of these swaps is a direct bolt-on job, with no welding or fabrication required. The only thing you have to watch out for is the driveshaft length, because the pinion length varies between the different stock axles. You can sometimes use the donor vehicle's driveshaft, or you can buy a new driveshaft that is the correct length. Be sure that the rear axle you are swapping has the same gear ratio as your front end, otherwise you may damage the transfer case and/or driveshafts.

Some MJ Comanches also came with Dana 44 rear axles that are nearly identical to the XJ's Dana 44.

This is a Dana 44 rear axle out of an XJ at the junkyard. This is a direct bolt-on swap for any other XJ with the exception of possibly the stock driveshaft. Dana 44s out of the Jeep Comanches can also be swapped, but Comanches are spring under, so the leaf spring perches will need to be relocated to the top of the axle tubes.

The only difference is that the spring perches are on the bottom of the axle tubes because the MJ is sprung under (leaf springs mount to the bottom of the axle). The spring perches need to be relocated to the top of the axle tube and welded.

Using a Ford 8.8-inch rear end out of a 1995 or newer Ford Explorer is also a popular rear axle swap. The advantages are that it comes with 31-spline shafts; some later models have disc brakes and stock 4.10:1 gears. These axles are about 3/4 inch narrower per side than stock XJ axles, so you most likely want to add wheel spacers to widen the track. The spring perches need to be relocated, and there have been reports of tubes spinning in the center section, so the tubes should be welded to prevent that from happening.

Some Ford 9-inch, Dana 60, or even Chevy 14-bolt rear axles are also good candidates for swapping, but they require fabrication and welding.

Choosing a Gear Ratio

After putting on those big tires, your Jeep may feel sluggish and might not have the same "get-up-and-go" that it used to. Your gas mileage has probably taken a turn for the worse, too. Well, forget about engine modifications right now. What you need is new gears!

Just like a 10-speed bicycle, the different-size sprockets, or gears, have a direct relationship to how hard it is to turn the pedals. With the chain on the smaller sprocket of the rear wheel, it is harder to get going, but once you reach cruising speed you don't need to pedal as much. Your Jeep is similar, only instead of a smaller sprocket, you increased the diameter of your tires. The effect is

Dustin's Jeep gets an axle swap. He's about to pull out his Dana 35 and put in an MJ Dana 44 with relocated perches and raised shock mounts. It also has 4.56:1 gears and a locker.

the same. It takes more energy to get up to speed, but once you're there (highway speeds, for example), you'll be cruising along at a lower engine RPM. In this case, you are likely out of the engine's power band, and as a result you notice the automatic transmission kicking out of overdrive on any kind of incline just to maintain speed. Not only does it give you worse gas mileage, it's also harder on your engine and transmission.

Changing the ring-and-pinion inside the axles, or re-gearing, helps restore your power on take-off and bring the cruising speed back into the engine's power band. Re-gearing also benefits you off-road by lowering your crawl ratio. Your crawl ratio is how slowly you can go, as determined by your lowest transmission gear ratio, your transfer case's low-range ratio, and your axle gear ratio.

Swapping gears is precision work and requires special tools. It is a job usually left to a professional gear installer, because screwing up a gear installation may result in noisy gears or worse, a grenaded differential. Because re-gearing is a rather expensive modification, it's usually some-

thing that you only want to do once, so have it planned out according to your desired tire size. For example, many people do not re-gear with 31-inch tires because they plan to go bigger in the future. It is also cost-efficient to install lockers at the same time as the gear work, rather than paying again later to have your locker installed.

As a general rule, stock gearing is 3.55:1 for XJs with the 4.0L and automatic transmission; it's 3.07:1 for XJs with the 4.0L and manual transmission. XJs with the 2.5L 4-cylinder

Re-gearing the axles means changing the ring and pinion to a different ratio. The number of teeth on the ring gear and pinion gear determine what ratio it will have. These are stock gears from a Chrysler 8.25-inch axle with a 3.55:1 ratio.

engine have 4.10:1 gears. Ratios of 3.73:1 and 4.56:1 were also used in some Cherokees, usually with a towing or off-road package. If you're not sure what you have, there are ways to verify your gear ratio. One is to jack up the Jeep, put it in neutral, and turn a wheel by hand, counting the revolutions of the wheel in comparison to the revolutions of the driveshaft (ratio). You can also open the differential cover and divide the number of ring gear teeth by the number of pinion gear teeth. Or, if you are really lucky, the gear ratio is stamped on the cover somewhere or on a tag around the axle tube, as is the case with the Chrysler 8.25s. This is assuming that the gears haven't been changed by the previous owner.

Your gear choice is best based on your tire size. Because the numbers represent a ratio (for example, 3.55:1) higher numbers mean lower gears, and that's what you want: low gears.

Depending on your stock gear ratio, you may also need to swap in a new differential carrier to accommodate the new gears. This is because a given carrier is meant for a certain range of gear ratios (higher or lower), and your desired ratio may fall outside that range. For example, when going from 3.55:1s to 4.10:1s, you need a new carrier for the Dana 30, but you could keep your existing carrier in a Dana 35 or Chrysler 8.25.

Carrier Height

Axle	Lower / Higher Carrier
Dana 30	3.55 & down / 3.73 & up
Dana 35	3.31 & down / 3.55 & up
Dana 44	3.73 & down / 3.92 & up
Chrysler 8.25	2.56 & up use same carrier

Manual Hub Conversion

Both Warn and MileMarker make a manual hub conversion for the Dana 30 axle. Although these kits may cost more money than some people like to dump into a Dana 30, they are a great upgrade if you plan on keeping the axle.

Stock hubs are non-serviceable, and when they go bad they are expensive to replace. Because the stock hubs cannot be unlocked, the axle shafts, differential gears, and front driveshaft are always turning even though 4WD is not engaged. Over time, this causes wear. With manual hubs unlocked, the shafts,

This conversion requires cast rotors (not composite) with a 1/4-inch-thick mounting flange. The holes in the center of the rotors need to be machined to a diameter of 3.575 inches. I took the rotors to a machine shop to have them machined and also had the shop press on the wheel studs into the hubs. Be aware that this kit also spaces the wheels out about .75 inch on each side.

gears, and driveshaft no longer spin in 2WD, which not only eliminates the wear and tear, but you don't have to worry about vibrations if you have issues with your front driveline. In theory, without the drag from the front driveline, gas mileage should

Tire and Gear Chart

Tire Size (inches)	Optimal Gears
31	4.10:1
32	4.56:1
33	4.56:1
35	4.88:1
37	5.13:1
39+	5.38:1

The Warn front hub conversion for the Dana 30 looks complicated based on the number of included seals and bearings. Warn makes two conversion kits: one for the stock bolt pattern using 5-on-4.5-inch hubs (shown here), while the other conversion uses the larger 5-on-5.5-inch premium hubs.

Removing the stock unit hubs and shafts isn't all that difficult, but I'm happy knowing that with the hub conversion, I'll never have to do this out on the trail.

I ran into a problem pressing in the Spicer 5-760x U-joints into the Warn shafts. The tolerances on these Warn shafts are very precise, so getting the U-joints in is more difficult than it appears. I shattered the cap of this joint trying to press it in. I think a needle bearing fell sideways and the cap bottomed out on it when I tried to press it in.

improve, but for most people, the increase is not noticeable. There are benefits for the trail as well. With manual hubs, if you ever have problems such as a broken U-joint, shaft, or gears, you can simply unlock the hubs, drive out in 2WD, and fix the problem in the comfort of your garage rather than on the trail. If the hub breaks on the trail and you have a spare (which you should), replacing it is as easy as changing a flat tire.

Limited-Slip Differentials

Some XJs came with a limited-slip differential, called the Trac-Lok, in the rear axle as a factory option, but they can also be added as an aftermarket upgrade. A differential without any traction device is referred to as an "open" differential; it allows the wheels to vary in speed as the Jeep turns a corner. The disadvantage to having open differentials is that when one wheel loses traction, it continues to spin while the other wheel has no power going to it at all. A limited-slip differential keeps some

The job took longer than expected due to the U-joint problem, but it turned out great. The experience you gain doing a project like this yourself is invaluable.

power to both wheels even if one begins to slip. Limited slips use clutch packs in the differential to transfer torque to wheels with the most traction. But they need some resistance to work, so if one wheel loses complete traction, such as if the wheel comes up off the ground, the limited slip acts like an open differential and all power goes to that wheel. Limited

slips can be very helpful when extra traction is needed, but true to their name, they are limited in how much traction they can provide under varying circumstances. Because limited slips allow differentiation of wheel speeds, they are very street-friendly traction devices.

If you think you have a Trac-Lok but are unable to tell for sure, you can give your VIN to the dealer and he can tell if your XJ came equipped with one. If you have a limited-slip differential, don't forget to add the friction modifier at every gear oil change. This additive, which helps eliminate clutch chatter in limited slips, can be obtained from the Jeep dealer.

Lockers

A locker is the ultimate traction device. A locker keeps power to both wheels regardless of the terrain. Even if one wheel is completely off the ground, the other still has power. There are different types of lockers, and you should be aware of what those differences are before you buy.

Although not common for many XJ axles, a spool locks both axle shafts together 100 percent of the time with no differentiation. This means that cornering on the street makes the tires chirp and wear a little faster because they are forced to travel at the same speed, even when they're following different paths. Spools probably aren't for you if your XJ is a daily driver. Because they are fully locked all the time, they cause more stress to your axle than any other type of locker.

Automatic lockers, such as the Detroit locker, are much more common. When you send power to the rear wheels, the two axle shafts are locked. When you let off the gas, such as when making a turn for instance, the locker automatically unlocks itself so that it can differentiate. An automatic locker is okay for the street but may click or pop as it locks and unlocks itself. These noises, while normal, seem to be louder with the cheaper "lunch-box lockers," such as the LockRight locker, that only replace the side gears of the differ-

One reason I chose to use the smaller hubs is because I didn't want to have to change bolt patterns on the rear and I wanted the smaller hub to become the fuse (weakest link) if something in the front axle is going to break. Changing out a hub on the trail is a simple task. So far, with 33s and now 35s, I haven't had to replace a hub.

ential rather than the entire carrier. Sometimes driving on the street with a locker can take some getting used to, and some people report that they can be difficult to handle in snow or icy conditions.

One misconception is that an automatic locker in the front axle affects on-road handling. This is not true because, in 2WD, there is no power to the front differential. The parts are still turning, but the locker is not locked. At worst, you may hear ratcheting or clicking sounds when cornering, but as stated above, these sounds are normal for most automatic lockers. Overall, automatic lockers are great off road because they provide consistent traction and you never have to wonder if they are engaged or not.

Selectable lockers are also available. As the term suggests, a selectable locker allows the driver to select when it is locked and when it is open. Selectable lockers are activated by air,

This is an open differential, meaning that it doesn't have a traction device such as a limited slip or a locker. With an open differential, if one tire starts to spin, all the power goes to that wheel. When that happens, the other wheel stops turning, so now neither wheel on that axle is providing any traction.

This is a Detroit locker. It's an automatic locker, so when your foot is on the gas, the shafts are locked together. When the axle is not under power, it unlocks.

cable, or electricity depending on the locker. Air-activated lockers include the ARB and Yukon's Zip locker. A manual cable activates the Ox locker. Electric lockers are available from Eaton and Auburn Gear.

For *Project Rubicon*, I decided to use ARB lockers due to their solid reputation and the fact that I was already planning to build an onboard air system. The ARB for my 29-spline 8.25 was installed in mid-2004 and has operated flawlessly, including two trips through the Rubicon. Even though a lunch-box locker would have been fine for my front end with the hub conversion, I was so happy with my rear ARB that I decided to put one in my Dana 30 as well. The thing that I really like about the ARB lockers is that when they're not engaged, they are just like an open differential, so I don't notice anything different in the way it handles on the street. But at the flip of a switch, the ARB lockers give me 100-percent locking capability, just like a spool.

A lot of opinions exist regarding whether you should add a locker to your front or rear axle first. Either way, a Jeep with one locker is far more capable than one without a locker. Add another locker and you will be amazed at what it can do. There are some things I would consider when adding a locker, and maybe this will help you decide which axle you want to lock. First of all, if you have a weak axle like the Dana 35, I would be hesitant to lock it because a locker adds a lot more stress. If you do lock it, carry

spare shafts. Also, driver finesse has a lot to do with axle breakage. If you have a heavy foot, or you are a "when in doubt, gun it" type of driver, the axle is under a lot more stress, especially when a locker is factored into the equation.

If you have a limited slip in one axle, consider adding a locker to the other one. Jeeps with one locker and one limited slip do exceptionally well, regardless of whether the locker is in the front or rear. Finally, I suggest looking long term. If you know that you will be upgrading to stronger axles in the future, I think it would be better to save your money and put it toward the axle you want.

The ARB selectable locker is more of a system than just a differential. Each ARB comes with everything needed except for the air source. When engaged, the ARB locker fully locks both axle shafts together. When it is turned off, the ARB acts just like an open differential with no hint that it's a locker.

The ARB switches are high quality and look great on the XJ dash or center console. With the compressor on, just flip the switch and it's locked.

Almost any air source can be used to operate the ARBs, but for ease of installation, nothing beats the ARB compressor. It includes a wiring harness with all the wires labeled and easy-to-use plug-in connections.

Jeep XJ Profile: Pete Montie's 1988 MJ Comanche

Pete's MJ has 5 inches of lift and 33-inch TrXus MT tires. The Dana 44 axle was swapped in as part of the 4WD conversion on this Comanche.

Year: 1988 Pioneer short bed
Engine: 4.0L I-6
Transmission: AX15 from a TJ
Transfer Case: NP231 from a TJ
Front Axle: High-pinion Dana 44
Rear Axle: Ford 9-inch
Gears: 4.10:1
Lockers: Front mini-spool, rear limited slip
Steering: Stock Dana 44
Suspension: 5-inch spring-over
Tires: 33 x 12.50–inch TrXus MT
Wheels: 15 x 8–inch, 5-on–5.5-inch bolt pattern

Pete's love affair with the Jeep Comanche began eight years ago when he got his first good job and with it his first long commute. Pete always wanted a 4WD Jeep, but felt a truck would better fit his lifestyle. That's when he discovered the Comanche pickup. The Comanche (MJ) was built by AMC from 1986 to 1992. The front half of the MJ is a unibody, and the engine and drivetrain are much the same as the XJ. The rear half of the MJ consists of a truck bed bolted down to a fully boxed frame. The bed can be removed from the truck, exposing the frame underneath. Long-bed and short-bed MJs were offered, and both have a longer wheelbase than the XJ. The short-bed MJ has a 113-inch wheelbase, while the long-bed is 119 inches. Some long-bed MJs came with the "Metric Tonne" or "Payload Package" designed for hauling. It included an AMC Model 20 rear axle in 1986 or the Dana 44 for 1987–1992, as well as heavy-duty springs and shocks. All MJs have a spring-under rear suspension; the leaf springs mount underneath the axle.

Jeep XJ Profile: Pete Montie's 1988 MJ Comanche *CONTINUED*

The rear axle was also swapped out for this Ford 9-inch. The leaf springs were moved from the stock "spring-under" location to above the axle, or "spring-over."

Sometimes longer-wheelbase trucks have stiffer suspensions that don't flex well, but not Pete's Comanche! He can easily stuff a 33-inch tire into the wheel wells.

Pete wanted a 4WD, but he wasn't able to find one near him that fit his price range, so he settled on finding the necessities: 4.0L, stick, and air conditioning. When he found his 2WD 1988 Pioneer it was love at first sight. It was in need of some immediate TLC (front/rear windows, brakes, tires, exhaust, etc.), but none of that mattered to Pete. As problems came along, each repair was seen as a chance to upgrade. When the alternator seized, he got a 170-amp replacement. When the radiator went south, he replaced it with an XJ three-core unit with radiator cap. When the 3.07:1-geared Dana 35 began spitting teeth, he hunted down a Dana 44 with 3.54:1 gears. Failed battery? Optima! Exploded Peugeot transmission? AX-15!

Even when other owners might have dropped this MJ off at the scrap yard, Pete decided to transform it into the 4x4 of his dreams. The 2WD to 4WD conversion could have been a bolt-in job using MJ/XJ parts, but Pete wanted more of a challenge. He decided on 4.10:1-geared 1978 Ford half-ton axles from a full-size Bronco. Pete swapped in the high-pinion Dana 44 in front and kept the Ford

The custom work to the truck bed is functional and well designed. The roll bar ties into the rear bumper and includes a spare tire mount.

three-link radius-arm suspension, but built his own crossmember and adapters. The coil pads were relocated to sit 2 inches higher than stock, and Pete used 3-inch lift coils for a total gain of 5 inches. The rear axle is a Ford 9-inch. For the rear suspension, Pete went spring-over and used additional MJ leafs as AALs. With a total of 5 to 5.5 inches of lift and some fender trimming, there is room to stuff 33-inch TrXus MTs when it is flexed. There was also no need for an SYE, as the MJ's longer rear driveshaft isn't nearly as susceptible to vibration. For traction, Pete kept the original Ford posi-traction in the rear and added a mini-spool in front.

Once the truck was up and running, Pete installed 3 x 5–inch bumpers with built-in 2-inch receivers for recovery. Then he added a custom roll bar, tire carrier, T-case skid plate, and 2 x 2–inch rocker guards. A big tool and parts box, Hi-Lift jack, second battery, and a carbon dioxide tank found a home in the bed, but left plenty of room for camping gear. There is room under the bed to mount a complete set of spare axle shafts. Aside from a high-performance ignition, air filter, and muffler, the engine is stock. Horsepower is a bit lacking after more than 190,000 miles, so a stroker engine is in the works.

Pete's love of the MJ isn't limited to his own rig. He actively helps other Comanche owners find help online and has set up an MJ-specific site, ComancheClub.com. He also organizes the annual Comanche Pow-Wow in October at the Badlands Off-Road Park in Attica, Indiana. This year, Pete and his canine co-pilot Carly (who wears a safety harness when wheeling) went on a three-week, 3,000-mile dream vacation from Michigan to Moab, wheeling along the way with fellow Comanche owners in Illinois and Colorado. ■

Pete kept the Ford radius arms when he swapped in the front axle, but the crossmember is custom. Beefy rock rails protect the rocker panels.

Even though the MJ is not as common as the XJ, and has less aftermarket support, the MJ Comanche can still be built into a very capable off-roader.

TRANSFER CASES AND DRIVELINE

The transfer case delivers power to the front driveshaft when 4WD is selected; power always goes to the rear wheels. It also includes low-range gear reduction for more power in low-speed off-road situations. The transfer case is mated to the back of the transmission and has output shafts for both the front and rear driveshafts. The 2WD Jeeps do not have a transfer case. As described in Chapter 1, there are two 4WD systems: Command-Trac with the NP231 transfer case, which is part-time only for off-road driving, and Selec-Trac with the NP242 transfer case, which has both part-time and full-time modes. Full-time 4WD can be used on any surface, including dry pavement, because the Selec-Trac transfer case has a differential that controls torque transfer to the front and rear axles. Part-time 4WD in either the Selec-Trac or Command-Trac is not for use on any hard surface road (pavement), unless it is covered by snow or ice. With no differential, the driveshafts are forced to turn at the same rate, causing binding and possibly damaging your U-joints or transfer case.

The stock NP231 and NP242 transfer cases are built by New Pro-

The transfer case sends power to the front driveshaft when 4WD is engaged. It is a critical link to any 4WD system.

cess Gear, whose parent company is New Venture Gear, which is why, occasionally, the same transfer cases are shown as NV231 instead of NP231. These transfer cases are pretty decent units and are quite reliable, even though they sometimes get a bad rap for having an aluminum

case and being chain driven. When these cases fail, it is usually due to neglected maintenance, such as never changing or even checking the fluid. High range has a 1:1 ratio. Low range is 2.72:1, which isn't great, but if you have the rear axles re-geared appropriately for your tire size, the

This is the ID tag on all New Process transfer cases. It shows the transfer case model number (231 J) and low-range ratio (272, or 2.72:1). New Process transfer cases are used in many vehicles. The "J" in the model number means it was made for a Jeep vehicle.

This is the Selec-Trac 4WD shift lever with 1997 and newer trim. The Selec-Trac 4WD system has an optional full-time 4WD mode.

This is the 4:1 low-range reduction kit by TeraFlex. It replaces the front half of the NP231 transfer case.

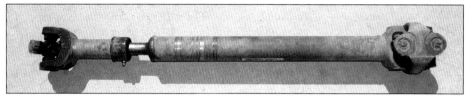

Transfer Case Specs		
Transfer Case	Maximum Torque Capacity (ft-lbs)	Approximate Gross Weight (pounds)
NV231	1,885	5,920
NV241	5,555	8,800
NV242	1,486	5,500

All 1987 and newer XJs use a Spicer double-cardan driveshaft, also referred to as a CV driveshaft.

2.72:1 reduction works well for most people. The higher reduction you have, the slower you are able to crawl over difficult obstacles or down steep descents.

Earlier-model Cherokees built prior to 1987 used slightly different versions of the New Process transfer cases. They were the NP207 Command-Trac and NP228 and NP229 Selec-Tracs. These transfer cases have slightly less low reduction, at 2.61:1.

Sometimes 2.72:1 low range just isn't low enough and you end up wanting 4:1. You have a couple of different options for 4:1 low range. One is to buy the TeraFlex 4:1 low-range kit for your NP231. Several other transfer-case swaps can give you lower than the stock 2.72:1, too. An NP241 Rock-Trac transfer case, which is stock in the Wrangler TJ Rubicon, is almost a direct swap, as long as your transmission has the 23-spline output shaft. The Rock-Trac has 4:1 low range, it's stronger overall than the NP231 and NP242, and it even comes with a fixed yoke instead of slip yoke, so there's no need to buy a slip-yoke eliminator kit. Other potential swaps include the Atlas 2-speed or 4-speed transfer case from Advance Adapters, which comes in a variety of low-range ratios. StaK 4x4 is another company that makes 2- and 3-speed transfer cases.

To give you a comparison on the strength ratings of the stock NP231/242 versus the NP241, see the chart above for some figures from New Venture Gear's website, newventuregear.com.

This shows that the NP241 Rock-Trac is substantially stronger than the stock transfer cases. For reference, a stock 4WD XJ weighs approximately 3,400 pounds, while a built XJ loaded for the trail is probably a good 1,000 pounds heavier than that.

Front Driveshafts

All 1987 and newer XJs use a Spicer driveshaft with a single cardan (commonly called a U-joint) on the axle end and a double-cardan joint on the transfer-case end. This type of driveshaft is commonly referred to as a constant-velocity (CV) driveshaft, even though the double-cardan

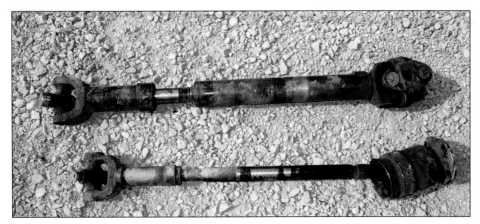

This photo compares the 1984–1986 GKN driveshaft (bottom) with the later Spicer driveshaft (top). The Spicer shaft is a much better piece.

The GKN (right) uses a true CV, or "constant velocity" joint, shown here compared to the Spicer double-cardan (left). If you have a GKN driveshaft, look into converting the yoke so you can use a Spicer driveshaft instead.

is technically not the same as a CV joint that is used in axle half-shafts on passenger cars. The stock Spicer driveshaft can be used up to 7 inches of lift or so, but if you have a low-pinion axle, you might run into length issues at slightly lower lift heights. If your front driveshaft is too short, a driveshaft shop can lengthen it or you can invest in a new shaft.

The 1984–1986 XJs came with weaker front driveshafts. Most of these early XJs have the GKN driveshaft with a true CV joint. It resembles a stick in a tin can bolted to the transfer case. To be honest, I don't think it's any stronger than a stick in a tin can, either! The CV joint on the GKN driveshaft doesn't like operating at steep angles, so if you have a tall lift, expect the CV joint to go bad very quickly. If you have one of these shafts, it would be worthwhile to change to a Spicer driveshaft. It's a straightforward conversion if you use a Spicer driveshaft yoke for the transfer case and a stock Spicer driveshaft that is the correct length. Stock driveshafts vary in length according to the engine and transmission that are used.

I have also seen another type of driveshaft used on these early XJs that resembles a smaller version of the Spicer double-cardan used on the 1987 and newer XJs. The yoke on the transfer case looks like a cross between the GKN tin can and the normal Spicer yoke. The diameter of the driveshaft tube is smaller as well. The few of these driveshafts I have seen looked like they were made by Spicer, but I cannot confirm that at this time. I imagine these driveshafts could be swapped out for the standard Spicer driveshaft and yoke just as easily if needed.

Rear Driveshafts

The stock rear driveshaft is one tube with a 1310 U-joint on each end. The slip yoke slides on the transfer case output shaft. Rear driveshaft length varies greatly among XJs. Because 2WD Cherokees don't have transfer cases, their driveshafts are very long. The 4WD Cherokee driveshafts

This is a standard 1310-size U-joint. This U-joint can be bought in either greasable or non-greasable versions.

The rear driveshaft is one tube with a U-joint on each end. The slip yoke is connected to the front U-joint and slides onto the transfer case output shaft.

The transfer cases on pre-1996 XJs have an extension housing that covers the driveshaft's slip yoke. This housing adds support to the slip yoke, which is why these vehicles tend to have less vibration when lifted.

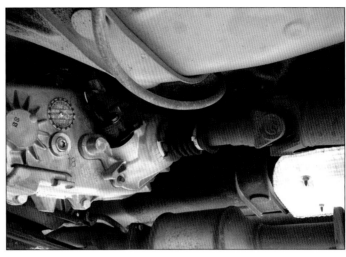

The 1996 and newer XJs lack the extension housing of the earlier models. Because there is less support between the output-shaft bearing and the driveshaft U-joint, this design is more prone to developing vibrations when the angle of the driveshaft increases, such as after you install a lift kit.

also vary greatly depending on the transmission and rear axle. As mentioned below in the section on slip yoke eliminators, you need to swap out this shaft if you are installing a SYE. You need a CV driveshaft.

Slip Yoke Eliminators

Lifting a Cherokee results in steeper driveshaft angles, which can sometimes lead to driveline vibration. Some XJs are more prone to vibration than others, and there's no way to know for certain if you'll get them until your Jeep is actually lifted. 1996 and newer XJs are more prone to vibration than older ones due to a change in the slip-yoke design. Pre-1996 XJs have an extension housing on the back of the transfer case that encloses the slip yoke. This housing offers more support to the transfer case output shaft and is less likely to develop vibration at smaller lift heights. The 1996 and newer XJs do not have the extension housing, which means less support for the shaft. This makes them more sensitive to steeper driveshaft angles, and some newer XJs develop vibration with as little as 3 inches of lift. Some lift kits include a transfer-case drop to lessen the driveline angle, but this is really just a cheap band-aid fix that may or may not work. Besides, why give up clearance by lowering the transfer case just after lifting the Jeep to gain clearance? The real solution is a slip yoke eliminator kit, or SYE for short. These are also referred to as a fixed yoke conversion or short-shaft kit.

A heavy-duty SYE kit replaces the stock output shaft with a thicker and

A transfer-case drop lowers the crossmember that supports the transmission and transfer case in an effort to reduce the driveline angle. The big downside is that it reduces clearance under the vehicle and makes the transfer case more vulnerable.

Left: This is a heavy-duty SYE made by Advance Adapters. Notice the beefy output shaft that will replace the stock shaft in the transfer case. Right: This shows the Advance Adapters SYE installed on a 1996 XJ. Not only did it eliminate the slip yoke on the output shaft, but in addition, the driveshaft joint is much closer to the transfer case.

shorter output shaft with either a fixed yoke or driveshaft flange. Having a shorter output shaft also means the distance between the yoke or flange and the rear differential is increased, which lessens the angle of the driveshaft. The yoke or flange is also closer to the bearing that supports the shaft. This results in less vibration as well as less stress on the output shaft bearing. Advance Adapters, JB Conversions, Rubicon Express, and oth-

ers offer HD SYE kits for the NP231. Installation can be done without removing the transfer case from the Jeep, but some prefer to remove it to make the SYE kit easier to install.

Not only does Rubicon Express offer a HD SYE, but it also makes a different version of SYE that doesn't require you to open the transfer case to swap the shaft. This kit, affectionately called the "hack-n-tap," is installed by cutting the stock

This is the Rubicon Express "hack-n-tap" SYE, which has been in use on Project Rubicon *for more than three years without problem. The CV shaft bolts to a flange on the output shaft.*

output shaft to shorten it, drilling a hole in the center of it, and tapping threads so that a driveshaft flange can be bolted on. As long as it's installed properly, the hack-n-tap SYE works well. Even though it may not be as strong as a HD SYE kit, the hack-n-tap is still stronger than the stock driveline.

The hack-n-tap is a low-cost alternative for 1996 and newer XJs, as it's roughly $150 cheaper than a HD SYE. However, the hack-n-tap costs more for the pre-1996 XJs, so in this case, you are better off getting an HD SYE instead. If you have the NP242 transfer case, there are fewer SYE kits to choose from, so the hack-n-tap is a good option for you as well. Don't forget: With any SYE kit, you need a new CV driveshaft to go with it.

Long-Travel Yokes

A few companies advertise long-travel yokes as being an alternative to an SYE. Many people believe that because their driveshaft is too short after a lift, a long-travel yoke is the solution. This is not true, and I

You'll need a new driveshaft with any SYE kit. This is a typical aftermarket CV driveshaft.

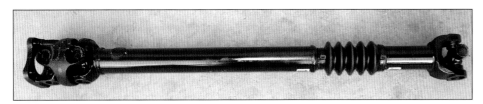

This is a rear CV driveshaft from High Angle Driveline. It has a flange mount on the CV end.

think the term "long-travel" is misleading. Here is what a long-travel yoke is used for: On some lifted XJs, the driveshaft angle is steep enough that as the driveshaft turns, the slip yoke ears make contact with the driveshaft. This binding causes a clunking sound that is sometimes quite loud, especially when taking off from a stop. In severe cases, this condition is pretty obvious, but if you're not sure, check for rubbing marks on the yoke ears. A long-travel yoke (which is simply a stock YJ yoke) has less interference between the ears and can therefore be used with a driveshaft at steeper angles. Another solution is to grind away metal from the yoke ears to create clearance. I'm not so sure I like this idea because the yoke ears may be weakened.

Installing an SYE gives you the same benefits as the long-travel yoke

because the angle between the yoke and driveshaft are split between the two U-joints of the CV joint instead

of just one. The SYE is better because the output shaft is shortened, creating more distance between the end of the shaft and the rear axle. This distance lessens the angle of the driveshaft and lessens the angles of the two U-joints. You can take the cheap way out and use the long travel yoke if this binding is the only problem you have, but I prefer to do it right the first time and install the SYE.

Shims

You can rotate the rear axle by inserting shims between the leaf packs and the spring perch. This can help you set your pinion angle to avoid vibrations. Shims are available in different angles; 2-, 4-, and 6-degree shims are the most commonly used shims for XJs. Make sure that when you add shims they are bolted to the bottom of the leaf pack using a new center pin. Also, it is better to use steel shims rather than aluminum, as the aluminum shims have been known to crack.

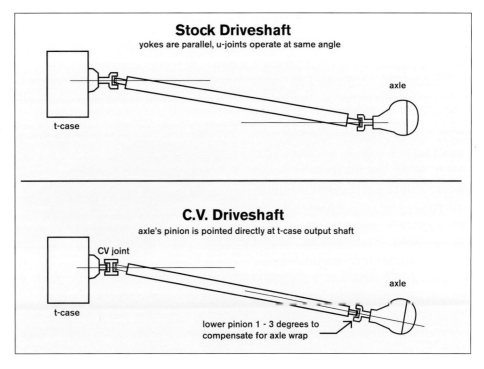

Measuring Driveline Angles

To prevent driveline vibration after an SYE is installed, the pinion should be set between 1 and 3 degrees lower than the driveshaft angle. I set the angles shown by using 4-degree shims. Your setup may require different shims, which is why it is important to actually take these measurements rather than guessing or "eye-balling" what you think is correct. My shims set the pinion 1 degree less than the driveshaft. This was within the 1- to 3-degree range and operates perfectly without any vibrations. ■

The most accurate way to obtain the pinion angle is to place the angle finder on the pinion yoke. In this case, the pinion measures 13 degrees from vertical (90 – 77).

The driveshaft angle can be obtained by placing the angle finder on the driveshaft. In this case, the driveshaft is at 14 degrees.

After the SYE and CV driveshaft are installed, the goal in shimming your axle is to point the pinion up toward the transfer case. In theory, the pinion yoke and driveshaft should be directly in line with each other, at zero angle. However, because of the leaf springs, axle wrap may occur, pushing the pinion up when the Jeep is accelerating. To compensate for this, the pinion should be lowered 1 to 3 degrees. Many people just throw in 4-degree shims and call it good by eyeballing the pinion angle. That's fine if it works, but if you end up with vibration, it's easy to measure your angles using an inexpensive angle finder. At first I just eyeballed mine, which was fine until I re-geared. The driveshaft was spinning at a much higher RPM than before, which caused a humming sound because my pinion was too low. I measured the angle between the pinion and driveshaft and figured that I needed a 6-degree shim instead of the 2-degree shims I was using at the time.

One thing to be aware of when using shims, especially 6 degrees or more, is that the pinion may be pointed so far up that the pinion bearing might not be getting enough lubrication. Without shims, the factory recommendations are to fill the differential up to the bottom of the fill hole, but with the pinion pointed up, you aren't able to get enough gear oil into the differential for proper lubrication. You can try parking on a downward slope when fill-

Shims are angled pieces of metal used to adjust the rear pinion angle. They come in varying degrees of slope, with 2, 4, and 6 being common for XJs.

ing the differential, or overfill it on level ground to get the right amount of gear oil in. I do this by covering most of the fill hole with my thumb, inserting the tip of the gear oil bottle, and squirting in more. I pull my thumb away and quickly replace the fill-hole plug before too much spills back out.

This shows a 6-degree shim used to tilt the rear pinion upward. It was securely attached to the bottom of the leaf pack with a new center pin; it was not just sandwiched between the leafs and spring perch.

Jeep XJ Profile: Jason West's 1995 XJ, *Big Red*

Jason's **Big Red** *has been an icon in the XJ community since back in the day when 3-inch lifts and 31-inch tires were considered big for a Cherokee. Today,* **Big Red** *sits on 35s. (Photo Courtesy Jason West)*

Year: 1995
Engine: 4.0L I-6
Transmission: AW4 4-speed automatic
Transfer Case: NP231 with SYE and 2LO kit
Front Axle: TJ Dana 30
Rear Axle: Dana 44
Gears: 4.56:1
Lockers: ARB front, Detroit rear
Steering: OffRoadOnly U-Turn cross-over
Suspension: RE 5.5-inch short-arm lift
Shocks: Bilstein 5150
Tires: 35 x 12.50–inch Goodyear MT/R
Wheels: 15 x 8–inch Rockcrawlers with 3.75-inch backspacing

Jason got the Jeep (nicknamed *Big Red* by his father) brand new back in the summer of 1995 mainly as a camp-ing vehicle and a tow rig for his ski boat. In October 1996, he attended his first Jeep Jamboree (the Ouachita Jeep Jamboree in Hot Springs, Arkansas) and immediately got hooked on off-roading. Jason installed his first lift kit the following summer, and he hasn't stopped wrenching on it. A lot has changed over the years, with *Big Red* going through various stages of upgrades, from 3.5 inches of lift and 31s to 5.5 inches and 35s.

The Jeep's engine has been modded with a Jeepers and Creepers bored-out throttle body and heavy-duty bat-tery cables, Poweraid throttle-body spacer, Airaid reusable air filter in the stock airbox, TurboCity high-flow thermostat housing, GDI 3-core radiator, Optima red-top battery, and a B&M tranny cooler. The exhaust duties are handled by a Borla header, DynoMax high-flow catalytic converter, and a Flowmaster 50-Series cat-back system.

Jeep XJ Profile: Jason West's 1995 XJ, *Big Red* CONTINUED

The front of Jason's rig sports a Custom 4x4 Fabrication bumper, Warn winch with synthetic winch rope, and Light Force 170 off-road lights. (Photo Courtesy Jason West)

Steering duties are handled by Off Road Only's U-Turn cross-over steering system. The bolt-on U-Turn kit doesn't require you to relocate the track bar. (Photo Courtesy Jason West)

The transfer case has a JB Conversions SYE kit, and a TeraFlex 2LO (one of Jason's favorite mods). A TeraFlex 4:1 low-range kit is in the plans.

The suspension is a Rubicon Express 5.5-inch Extreme Duty kit with Bilstein 5150 shocks front and rear. JKS sway bar disconnects let the front end flex out off-road, while Daystar extended poly bumpstops and DPG adjustable bumpstop plates keep the tires in check and the shocks from bottoming out. A scratched-up set of BushWacker flares keeps the 35-inch Goodyear MT/R tires covered and keeps the body (mostly) clean on the road.

Big Red has a TJ Dana 30 axle up front loaded with 4.56:1 gears, an ARB air locker, and a Warn 5 x 4.5 manual hub kit. An ARB air compressor is mounted in the storage area underneath the rear bench seat to provide the air to his front ARB locker. Steering is handled by an OffRoadOnly U-Turn cross-over system. The rear Dana 44 is out of a 1987 Cherokee and has matching 4.56s and a Detroit locker; one of these days it'll get some disc brakes.

The Jeep's armor consists of front and rear bumpers from Custom 4x4 Fabrication, rocker guards from Rocky Road Outfitters, rear Gila Monster quarter panel guards from Rock Lizard Fabrication, a front Custom 4x4 Fabrication differential cover guard, and door panel armor from Performance Metal Works. A full belly skid from DPG Off-Road protects the crossmember and transfer case, while a Skid Row skid plate guards the gas tank. The stock plastic taillights have also been replaced with a set of steel housings and LED lights from Farm Boy Designs.

A set of red and black Wet Okole seat covers and electroluminescent gauge overlays give the interior a bit of a sporty look, while a Clarion mini-disc head unit, XM radio, and an iPod Mini make sure that good tunes are never in short supply. Navigation on- and off-road is handled with a Garmin eMap GPS unit.

Other modifications consist of a Warrior Products safari rack, IPF headlights, LightForce 170 off-road lights with amber filters, Warn XD9000i winch loaded with MasterPull synthetic winch rope, lots of recovery gear, a set of PowerTank carbon dioxide tanks, Staun tire deflators, Cobra 75WXST CB, a custom hydraulic hood strut setup, Husky Liner floor mats, Raingler cargo net, and many other goodies.

Jason also started his website, Jeepin.com, in 1996 as a place to put write-ups, reviews, and photos online. The site has grown beyond Jason's wildest dreams to become one of the most popular Jeep-enthusiast sites on the web. In 2002, Jason and his wife started their own aftermarket parts business to go with the site.

Jason has had a lot of great adventures in his Jeep, including attending two Jeep Jamborees and two Camp-Jeep events, a wheeling trip to Colorado, numerous wheeling and camping trips in Arkansas and Texas, and one fateful jump that resulted in a bent front axle housing, three bent fenders, and a slight (but permanent) twist in the unibody.

Jason has met lots of great people over the years through Jeeps and off-roading, and that includes his wife. They actually met on a trail (yes, she has her own Jeep!) while they were riding with friends. They instantly hit it off and have been together ever since. ■

Big Red *flexes well and there's just enough room to stuff 35s with 5.5 inches of lift and trimmed fenders. (Photo Courtesy Jason West)*

Check out the Custom 4x4 Fabrication rear bumper, tire carrier, and lower rear quarter panel guards by Rock Lizard Fabrications as well as LED taillights and housings from Farm Boy Designs. (Photo Courtesy Jason West)

ENGINE AND TRANSMISSION UPGRADES

My goal with this book is to show how to make the Cherokee more capable off-road. Most XJ owners couldn't care less what the quarter-mile time is at the track, and you would never race that Honda sitting at the stoplight; you'd rather use it as an RTI ramp. If you have the 4.0L engine, you have plenty of power, so your focus should first be on the suspension, gears, lockers, protection, and recovery: things that really make a difference off-road. With all that being said, who couldn't use a little more power?

The 2.5L I-4 Engine

The 2.5L I-4 is a lightweight 4-cylinder engine that is similar to its big brother the 4.0L, except that it has two fewer cylinders. The 2.5L engine can be found in every year of the XJ except the 2001 model. It may not have a lot of power, but XJs with the 2.5L engine came with a 4.10:1 gear ratio in the axles to make up for it. This engine is durable and has no widespread reliability issues.

The 2.8L V-6 Engine

The GM-built 2.8L 60-degree V-6 is the same engine used in the Chevy S-10s and other vehicles. This 6-cylinder engine doesn't have a lot of power, and many of them suffer from reliability issues. It's no wonder Jeep ditched it in favor of the 4.0L I-6 after three years. If you're looking to swap in a more powerful engine, the 2.8L can be replaced by a GM 60-degree 3.4L engine from the Camaro. The 2.8L and 3.4L have the same exterior dimensions, making it an ideal swap. The primary difference between the two is on the inside: stroke and bore size.

I won't say it's impossible to swap in a 4.0L I-6 in place of the 2.8L V-6, but it is difficult. I have been told that the firewall was moved back in 1987 to make room for the 4.0L. Also, V-8s have been swapped in, but are uncommon due to the small engine compartment. You also have to ask yourself if it's worth it to swap in such a heavy engine, when the

Stock Engine Specs (does not include Diesel engines)		
1984–1986 Engines		
2.5L I-4 (carb)	105 hp @ 5,000 rpm	132 ft-lbs torque @ 2,800 rpm
2.5L I-4 (TBI)*	117 hp @ 5,000 rpm	135 ft-lbs torque @ 3,500 rpm
2.8L V-6	115 hp @ 4,800 rpm	145 ft-lbs torque @ 2,400 rpm
* 1986 only		
1987–1990 Engines (Electronic Fuel Injection)		
2.5L I-4	121 hp @ 5,000 rpm	135 ft-lbs torque @ 3,500 rpm
4.0L I-6	177 hp @ 4,750 rpm	220 ft-lbs torque @ 4,000 rpm
1991–1995 Engines (Multi-Port Fuel Injection)		
2.5L I-4	130 hp @ 5,250 rpm	139 ft-lbs torque @ 3,250 rpm
4.0L I-6 HO	190 hp @ 4,750 rpm	220 ft-lbs torque @ 4,000 rpm
1996–2001 Engines (Multi-Port Fuel Injection)		
2.5L I-4	130 hp @ 5,250 rpm	139 ft-lbs torque @ 3,250 rpm
4.0L I-6 HO	190 hp @ 4,750 rpm	225 ft-lbs torque @ 3,000 rpm

3.4L V-6 is a good upgrade in power, is an easier swap, and gets far better gas mileage than the V-8.

The 4.0L I-6 Engine

The 4.0L engine first appeared in the Cherokee in 1987. It was the best thing that could have happened to the XJ, especially after the 2.8L engine. The 4.0L engine is an inline 6, so don't ever make the faux pas of calling it a "V-6"! The inline 6 has all six cylinders in line, and a V-6 has three cylinders on each side of the engine tilted outward, resembling the letter "V." The inline 6 is known for putting out lots of torque at lower RPM. That's what makes it the perfect engine for the Cherokee. With the lightweight chassis and 4.0L, the Cherokee has a great power-to-weight ratio, making it very peppy on the street and aggressive off-road. This engine, also called the 4.0L Power Tech, is very tough and reliable. It is not uncommon for it to see upwards of 250,000 miles without a rebuild, and many XJ owners have even reported more than 300,000 miles!

In 1991, Jeep added multi-port fuel injection, bumping the 4.0L by 13 hp and earning it the High Output designation. Jeep kept upgrading the 4.0L, and in 2000 they did away with the distributor and spark plug wires and went with the modern distributorless ignition. This distributorless design uses a coil rail over the spark plugs with three individual coils in the rail. Each coil fires two

The 4.0L I-6 is a powerful engine with lots of low-end torque. It was used between 1987 and 2001, with 1991 marking the start of the High Output 4.0s.

This is the coil rail on 2000 and 2001 4.0L engines with the distributorless ignition system. This modern version of the 4.0 has no distributor cap or spark plug wires.

spark plugs simultaneously. This is called a waste-spark system.

Somewhere along the way, Jeep stopped making the badges that read "High Output," but even though your late-model 4.0L doesn't have the badge, it's still the same High Output engine as before.

I've left the 4.0L engine in *Project Rubicon* mostly stock until just recently. I'm also not an engine performance guru, but for the rest of this chapter, I'll share what I've done and what my impressions are. If, after reading this chapter, you'd just like to stick to the popular cone filter and loud exhaust, it really won't hurt my feelings. Remember, it's your Jeep to do with as you please, and there's certainly more than one way to push (or pull) out a little more horsepower.

When the time comes for a rebuild, consider increasing the displacement of your engine up to 4.9 liters with a stroker. For detailed information on how to build a stroker engine, I recommend *Jeep Cherokee XJ Advanced Performance Modifications 1984–2001*.

Snorkels

Living in Nevada and building a Jeep mostly for rocks, I'll be the first to admit that the idea of installing a snorkel may seem a bit odd. My neighbors are either fully convinced that I have indeed lost my mind, or they are still trying to figure out what that thing is sticking out of the side of my Jeep. But I've always wanted one, and while there's nothing wrong with the homemade snorkel look as long as it works, I knew that the only snorkel I would be happy looking at on *Project Rubicon* was the ARB Safari Snorkel.

Originally designed for use in the Australian outback, the ARB Safari Snorkel is a great item to have no matter where you live. Believe it or not, there is water even in Nevada, and you never know when you might be caught in a flash flood.

The standard routing method for the snorkel air hose has it loop down in front of the tire and up through the bottom of the inner fenderwell. I knew this would be a problem with my big tires, so I chose to insert it through the side instead. From underneath, you can see my tire's rub marks in the fenderwell. The tire comes close to the hose, but there is no way it can contact the hose and damage it.

Even water that's not as deep as you think can flood your engine. In this situation, a steep entry into the water dips the front grill into the water. The stock airbox is right behind the driver-side headlight, which puts it closer to the water than it might be otherwise.

This is the real test of the ARB snorkel. Just a moment before this photo was taken, water was over the front of the hood, as can be seen by the water line on it. Venturing into water this deep is definitely not a good idea without a snorkel. On this crossing, the inside of my engine may have stayed dry, but the inside of my Jeep did not!

Other than the amusement factor of having a snorkel, I saw two potential benefits: fording capability and the ability to take in cold air. I've always heard that cold air flowing into the engine is better than hot air, because it is denser and makes more power. This may be true, but I didn't notice any dramatic difference in the amount of power after installing the snorkel. I may have picked up more power if I'd already upgraded the exhaust, but at that point I was still using the stock muffler.

Regardless of any power gains from the snorkel, the real benefit is the fording capability. Being able to cross deep water without hydrolocking the engine is a pretty cool thing! Engines don't like water because water can't be compressed the way air can. When water enters the combustion chamber, the pistons still try to compress it, but can't, and that's where things get ugly (hydrolock). The results can be bent connecting rods, broken connecting rods, connecting rods protruding out of your oil pan, and sometimes even a cracked engine block. With a snorkle, the intake opening is at the roofline, so the chance that you'll suck in water is greatly diminished.

A few trails in the Sierras have water crossings, and it just so happens that the last winter produced record snowfall depths, so the rivers were very deep with all the snowmelt. I was heading off to do the Rubicon Trail with our local 4x4 club, and it turned out that the snorkel came in handy. Dozens of deep water holes were on the trail even though it was the end of June. Many of the crossings swallowed my 35-inch tires, so I knew the guys with 31s and less lift were probably pretty nervous. The snorkel gave me the peace of mind

Cone filters are very popular intake modifications. Getting rid of the stock air box can create room in the engine compartment for other things. The owner of this XJ mounted an air compressor and small air tank where his stock air box used to be.

that even if it were too deep to cross, at least the engine would be okay.

At one area of the trail, I found the ideal crossing to really test the snorkel. The line I chose took the XJ into water that lapped over the hood. Unfortunately, I hit a mound of sand and weeds that buried my front end, and I was hopelessly stuck in the middle of the 4-foot-deep river. Even with front and rear lockers I could not free the Jeep in forward or reverse. The engine never sputtered, but now with water filling the interior of the Jeep, I was afraid that the electronics would short out, so I shut off the engine. By the time I was winched out, water had risen to the top of the center console, and there were puddles of water on the front seats, getting deeper by the second.

After lamenting over my plush 2000 interior and scooping out as much water as I could, I started up the engine, still confident that the

intake was dry. I was less than pleased with my wet interior, but I couldn't have been happier with the way the snorkel performed! If I had tried the same crossing without a snorkel, I would be looking at a very expensive engine rebuild. I knew my next modifications would be Herculining the interior and adding more drain plugs!

One warning about getting stuck in deep water: When possible, it's best to keep the engine running. Otherwise, water flows in through the

tailpipe and could possibly reach the engine. In my case, I was okay because where I was stuck the engine was not fully submerged, and we got the Jeep out quickly. Water did get into my muffler but not up into the engine. If you are in a similar situation, and decide to turn the engine off, the safest thing to do once you get it up on dry land is to pull the spark plugs and crank the engine. This safely expels any water that made it into the cylinders. It's also a good idea to change the oil on the spot, assuming you are prepared to do so. Be aware that water may have gotten into the transmission also. Once you get it home, you want to change all the fluids, including the differential fluid.

Cowl Intake

After seeing Bryan Vetrano's intake, which he relocated into the passenger-side cowl, I decided I wanted the same thing on *Project Rubicon*. Actually, there was more to it than just that. I was also designing my hybrid-style roll cage and the ARB snorkel was in the way. The cowl intake was the perfect solution because it retains the advantages of a snorkel for deep-water fording (at least higher than the stock intake does), provides a source for cold air, and frees up space in the engine compartment.

Parts List		
Item	**Source**	**Cost**
Airaid cone filter	Summit (PN AID-700-430)	$31.95
3.0-inch OD exhaust pipe	Summit (PN SUM-640030)	$12.95
3.0-inch ID connector	Summit (PN WLK-41892)	$15.95
3.0-inch x 30-inch Spectre flex tube	Summit (PN SPE-8741)	$25.99
3.0-inch black ABS pipe	Home Depot	$5.00
Miscellaneous hose fittings and clamps	Home Depot	$10.00

The cowl is the hollow area between the dash and the engine compartment. The windshield wiper motor is inside the driver-side section of the cowl. The HVAC system draws air from the passenger-side section of the cowl, which is almost empty. With the cowl grill removed, the driver's side is open (for air to enter) but the passenger's side is not open on the top (to prevent water from entering the HVAC duct).

I chose this Airaid cone filter because of its dimensions. It has a 3½-inch flange, 4⅝-inch base, 3½-inch top, and is 7 inches long. It fits just inside the cowl, but it isn't too small either. I mounted it to a short section of 3-inch (ID) black ABS pipe because this pipe has an outside diameter of 3½ inches. Then, I added a short section of exhaust pipe to mount the flex hose.

The passenger-side cowl is an ideal location for the filter. However, to get it in there you need to cut a hole in the top. Even though the cowl is cut open, not much water can enter here because the cowl grill does not have any vent holes on that side.

It is a tight fit but the filter tucks nicely into the cowl.

Here is the flex hose entering the engine bay. I used a 3-inch hole saw for the opening and had to open the hole a bit more to accommodate the flex hose. A piece of rubber hose can be cut and fit around the opening to serve as a grommet to protect the flex hose.

Here is the rest of the hose going to the throttle body. The diameter of the exhaust coupler is exactly the right size to attach the stock accordion throttle-body tube. I welded the coupler in place but it was such a tight fit I think it would have been just fine without welding it. The CCV can be attached to the pipe with a hose fitting.

Air Filters

Replacing the stock air box and paper filter with a cone filter is a very common intake upgrade. K&N Engineering makes the most popular cone filter. A cone-shaped filter has more surface area, meaning more air can travel through it at a given time. Less resistance to airflow means more power and efficiency and better throttle response. Along with cone filters, K&N also manufactures replacement panel filters to fit inside the stock air box. K&N claims that its filters add horsepower and keep your engine cleaner. K&N filters have an oiled cotton media that can be cleaned and re-oiled when necessary, eliminating the need to keep buying disposable filters. This is especially handy for your Jeep, which probably gets dusty, dirty, or muddy more often than the average daily driver. You can also pick up a pre-filter that wraps around the cone filter and keeps big chunks of mud or dirt from becoming lodged in the filter. When you get home after a trail run, you just take off the pre-filter and rinse it out.

A large "filtration versus airflow" debate questions whether K&N filters adequately filter out particles that are small enough to pass through the filter, yet large enough that they may cause wear in the engine over time. The nay-sayers claim that a higher-flowing filter cannot give you better filtration. K&N claims that its filter maintains better airflow even as it gets dirty. At this time, I am still on the fence when it comes to using a K&N filter. I don't doubt that it produces some increase in horsepower, but whether or not it is better for the engine in the long term, I do not know.

One other consideration when using a cone filter is that it is more susceptible to damage since it has no air box to protect it. I saw a friend's cone filter become so clogged with mud that it was uncleanable and had to be replaced. Others have had the engine start to cut out when water has splashed onto the filter. Keep those issues in mind when you decide where to position the filter. You may decide that a couple of extra horsepower isn't worth the drama.

Bored-Out Throttle Body

The throttle body is like the mouth of the intake manifold. The wider this mouth can open, the more air that can be sucked in at one time. The problem with the stock throttle body is that it has a taper that restricts airflow. On *Project Rubicon*, the opening of the throttle body is 62 mm in diameter with a gradual taper down to 55 mm after the butterfly valve (or throttle plate). You can bore out the throttle body to remove the restrictive taper, which allows more air to pass through. A higher-flowing throttle body can help you pull more air through the air filter because there is no longer as much of a bottleneck behind it.

You can bore out your throttle body if you have the right equipment, or you can purchase one that has been bored out for you. Jeepers and Creepers of San Francisco is one company that bores out stock throttle bodies and uses the customer's throttle body as a core return. The throttle body I purchased from them was bored out to 60 mm at the bottom, which was a very visible 5-mm increase in diameter over stock. It was also very clean and polished, unlike the one on *Project Rubicon*, which I shamefully admit has never been cleaned.

The install was very simple and probably the only "bolt-on" modification I've done that truly was "bolt-on"! All you need to do is disconnect the sensors and unbolt the stock throttle body. Then bolt on the new one and

Boring out the throttle body increases the diameter of the opening for more airflow. You can see the difference between the stock body on the left (dirty) and the bored-out throttle body on the right.

plug the sensors back in. After disconnecting the battery to allow the computer to adjust to the new throttle body, it was ready for the first test.

I've always heard that this modification gives a better throttle response, and I would definitely agree. Of the performance modifications made so far, this one gave the biggest seat-of-the-pants improvement.

The bored-out throttle body measured 60 mm, which is a 5-mm increase over stock. This allows more air to flow through and into your engine.

Installing the new throttle body was easy. This shot shows the air hose moved out of the way, the throttle cables disconnected, and the three sensors unplugged. The stock throttle body is now ready to be unbolted from the manifold.

Aftermarket Exhausts

Realizing that more intake mods don't help me if there's nowhere for that air to go, I decided to turn my attention to the exhaust. My next modification was to trash the stock muffler and let the engine breathe easier through an aftermarket cat-back exhaust system. A cat-back exhaust system replaces everything from the catalytic converter back, which is the muffler and tailpipes.

I wanted a less restrictive exhaust, but I didn't want it to be obnoxiously loud, so I went with the DynoMax Super Turbo cat-back system. I'm always skeptical about companies' claims about their own product's performance, but I knew that the folks at rockcrawler.com had already independently tested this DynoMax kit. Installing it on an XJ with the 4.0L engine, they documented an increase of 6 hp and 8 ft-lbs of torque, verified on a third-party dynamometer. A dynamometer, or dyno, is a machine that uses resistance to monitor how much horsepower and torque your vehicle makes.

The DynoMax muffler and tailpipe bolted on very easily, with the muffler dimensions and pipe size being the same as stock, but I had to cut off the chrome tip because it was making direct contact with the extended shackles. It didn't break my heart to lose the chrome tip because, after all, "Chrome won't get you home," and I'm not going for the blingy look on my Jeep.

When the installation was complete, I took it for a test drive. My immediate impressions were that it wasn't loud at all; in fact, it didn't sound a whole lot different from stock. I can hear it slightly when

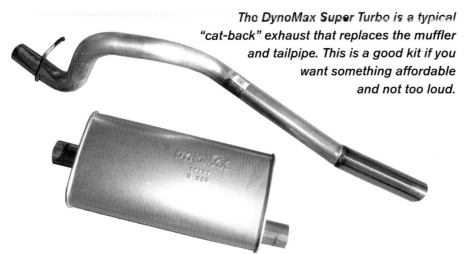

The DynoMax Super Turbo is a typical "cat-back" exhaust that replaces the muffler and tailpipe. This is a good kit if you want something affordable and not too loud.

under a hard acceleration. I am still debating whether or not I could actually feel a power increase. Of course the best thing to do would be to dyno test all these changes myself, but adding a few horsepower is not the focus of this book. Besides, it's already been tested and documented. That's good enough for me.

At this point, I've only upgraded part of the exhaust. For maximum power gains, an aftermarket header(s) and a high-flow catalytic converter can be added to complete the high-performance exhaust system. "Headers" are the aftermarket term for a tubular exhaust manifold. The stock exhaust manifold is notorious for cracking, and attempts at welding it often don't hold up for long. This makes upgrading to aftermarket headers even more appealing when you consider that stock replacement manifolds are expensive, especially for the 2000 and 2001 models. Banks, Borla, and Pacesetter manufacture aftermarket headers.

This is what the stock muffler looks like inside. The tubes in the muffler route the air in a way that keeps the exhaust quiet, but it also restricts flow. Aftermarket mufflers route the air through in a much less restrictive manner.

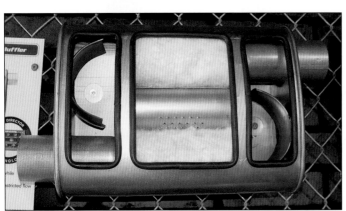

The DynoMax muffler has patented flow directors that reduce turbulence in the exhaust flow, making it less restrictive than the stock muffler. (Photo Courtesy Travis Thompson)

The DynoMax muffler mounted very easily. The only fitment problems I had was the tailpipe hitting the extended shackles and the pipe coming very close to the Tomken gas tank skid. That isn't DynoMax's fault though, as this system is intended to fit on a stock Cherokee.

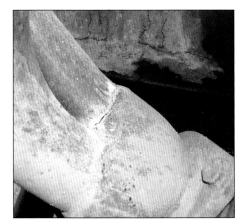

If you look closely, you'll see the crack in this exhaust manifold. Cracks like this are common, so instead of repairing it, you might consider upgrading to an aftermarket header.

Filter Cross-Reference List		
Brand	**Stock (PN)**	**Oversize (PN)**
AC Delco	PF13	PF2
Fram	PH16	PH8A
K&N Gold	HP-2004	HP-3001
Mobil 1	M1-204	M1-301
Motorcraft	FL332	FL1A
Napa Gold	1085	1515
Purolator	L14670	L30001
WIX	51085	51515

Using an Oversized Oil Filter

Using an oversized oil filter is a great idea for XJs with the 4.0L engine. For 1993 and newer models with the filter positioned horizontally, the filters screw right on with no modification necessary. If you have a 1987–1992 XJ that has the oil filter in the vertical position and metric threads, it is possible to convert to a horizontal position and use an oversized filter with SAE threads.

The biggest benefit to using a larger oil filter is the increased filtering capacity. The larger oil filters are about 1/3 taller than stock, which means roughly 33 percent more filtering media inside the filter. The ability to filter out and hold more contaminants means that the oil stays cleaner longer. I have also found it very convenient to use the larger size along with synthetic oil that can be used for extended periods of time. Even though synthetic oils can be used for longer intervals than conventional oil, the stock-size filter still eventually becomes full of contaminants. Once that happens, you aren't doing

the engine any good by keeping that dirty oil circulating through it. With the larger filter size, I use synthetic oil with a change interval of every 5,000 miles. The larger oil filter gets replaced at every interval along with the oil.

Another benefit of using the larger filter size is that it allows you to run more oil through the engine. *Project Rubicon* takes about 1/4 quart more oil than before, and while this isn't a substantial amount, it helps with the overall lubricating, spreads a given amount of contaminants

An oversize filter (Mobil 1) is approximately 1/3 taller than the OEM-size Fram filter shown here. With extra filtering media, the larger filter can take more dirt out of your oil before it fills up.

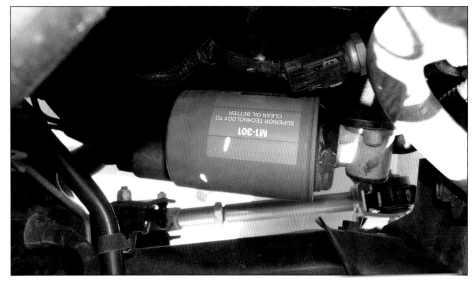

This view from the top of the engine shows the oversize oil filter mounted with plenty of room behind it. On 1993 and newer 4.0-liter engines where the oil filter is in the horizontal position, there are no modifications needed to use a larger filter.

over that much more oil, and helps keep the engine cooler.

What about oil pressure? There will not be any change in oil pressure by using a larger oil filter. The valving in the oversized filters is the same as stock sizes. However, I do like to add some oil to the filter before I screw it on so that it doesn't take quite so long for the filter to fill up when I first start the engine after the oil change.

If the above reasons haven't convinced you to use a larger oil filter yet, here's one more: the upgrade is free! The larger filter sizes cost the same amount as the stock sizes of the same brand, at least at the places I have shopped for filters. I can't think of a single reason not to run a larger filter, especially with the newer 4.0Ls that don't need any modifications. It's a great upgrade, and your engine will thank you for it!

Transmission Upgrades

Manual transmissions don't really need an auxiliary cooler, and there are not many upgrades that can or need to be done to them. Most guys with the Peugeot (BA10/5) transmission swap it out for an AX15 when the Peugeot goes bad. Parts for the Peugeot are simply too expensive and the AX15 is stronger, with its 23-spline output shaft (Peugeot has a 21-spline).

Automatic transmissions are much more sensitive to heat. Overheating an automatic transmission can cause it to fail, and transmission work isn't cheap. XJs with the towing package included an auxiliary transmission cooler, which was a small cooler mounted low on the grill in front of the radiator and air conditioning condenser. Most other XJs don't have an auxiliary cooler, but

This is the Peugeot BA10/5 transmission. It is surprisingly small and lightweight. The bolts near the top and bottom separate the two halves like a suitcase. Many enthusiasts replace the Peugeot transmission with an AX15 if it goes bad.

This is a very large Hayden transmission cooler mounted behind the grill. An auxiliary cooler can be extremely beneficial to automatic transmissions, which are more sensitive to excessive heat than manual transmissions.

their tranny lines are cooled as they pass through the driver-side tank of the radiator.

Installing an auxiliary cooler is not difficult and can definitely help keep the transmission temperatures down. Several aftermarket coolers are available from Hayden or B&M, or you could install the OEM (Mopar) auxiliary cooler if you can still buy it from a Jeep dealer or pick one up from a junkyard. Installing a transmission temperature gauge to go with it is a good idea.

Jeep XJ Profile: John Laurella's 1995 XJ, *The Badger*

The Badger *is one bad-ass XJ with 8 inches of lift and 36-inch IROKs on full-width axles. (Photo Courtesy John Laurella)*

Year: 1995
Engine: Jasper 4.0L I-6
Transmission: AW4 4-speed automatic
Transfer Case: NP231 w/AA SYE
Front Axle: Full-width Dana 44
Rear Axle: Full-width Dana 60
Gears: 5.13:1
Lockers: Detroit front and rear
Steering: Over-the-knuckle
Front Suspension: Rusty's 8-inch long-arm
Rear Suspension: Four-link with coil-overs
Tires: 36 x 13.50–inch IROKs
Wheels: 17 x 9–inch Allied RockCrushers

This bad-to-the-bone XJ is built for serious off-road use, but it wasn't always that way. In fact, it had a rough beginning. John purchased the Jeep from a woman he knew who was going to trade it in for $1,000 at the dealership. Why only

$1,000 for a 1995, you ask? Well first of all, it had 180,000 miles on it and it was blowing oil. The transmission pan was also leaking, and it just didn't look like it was well cared for. But John knew what he wanted to do with it and offered her the $1,000 to buy it.

Three months later, the transformation began. John took his XJ to a friend's shop where it was stripped bare inside and out. John sprayed the inside and underside with Dura-bak bed liner. He ordered a new Jasper 4.0 HO engine and sent the transmission out for a full rebuild. The transfer case was split open and an Advance Adapters SYE was installed. The stock Dana 30 and Chrysler 8.25 were stripped and rebuilt with Detroit lockers and 4.56:1 gears to compensate for the 35-inch Baja Claws.

To get this Jeep up in the air, John went with Rusty's Off-Road 8-inch long-arm kit. This kit was appealing for a couple of reasons. John liked the radius-arm geometry of the long-arms, plus they used factory bushings, which should

Jeep XJ Profile: John Laurella's 1995 XJ, *The Badger* CONTINUED

be easy to find if he needs to replace them down the road. With the tall lift, John knew he had to do something about the steering. He ordered the TeraFlex High Steer, which included the high-steer knuckle and AlumiBar drag link and tie-rod. John encountered bumpsteer with this setup because the track bar had not been raised level to the new drag link. But *The Badger* was being built as a trail rig to handle mostly mud, which New Jersey is known for. So, at the time, the little bit of bumpsteer was not an issue for John; this setup worked great for that terrain.

John moved to Utah, the "dreamland of the 4WD community" as he puts it, and that's where it all changed. He found that what it takes to wheel out West was completely different from back home. Within a few months, John broke a rear axle shaft that also took out the rear locker. A few weeks later, he broke a front axle joint, and at the same time took two

The front suspension is Rusty's 8-inch long-arm. The front axle is a full-width Dana 44 with over-the-knuckle steering. Rumor has it that John is working on a hydro-assist steering as one of his next upgrades. (Photo Courtesy John Laurella)

teeth off the ring gear. At that point, John knew what had to be done to deal with his driving style in the new environment: stronger axles! He found a set of 3/4-ton axles from a 1979 Ford. The front was a Dana 44, and the rear was a full-floating Dana 60. They were both stripped down and rebuilt with Detroit lockers and 5.13:1 gears. The rear axle received a set of disc brakes to help with stopping power.

John ordered new tires and rims to go with the new axles. He ordered 36-inch Super Swamper IROKs on 17-inch rims to help clear the brakes. And because the axles were full-width (wider than stock), he ordered the wheels with 5-inch backspacing to keep them from sticking out too far. To mount the front axle, John used a Rubicon Express bracket kit, slightly modified to accept the Dana 44 and the new steering. He went with over-the-knuckle steering, which was accomplished by using two high-steer arms on top of the Dana 44 flat-top knuckles. A new custom track bar mount was fabricated to move it above the axle to match the drag link. This steering produced no bumpsteer what-

soever, and John isn't even using a steering stabilizer. The front axle was also pushed forward 1.5 inches to re-center it in the wheel well.

John added a Rigidco front bumper for better approach angle and recovery. The rear bumper and tire carrier are homebrew and also include recovery points. Both bumpers have 2-inch receivers to work with a Warn 9.5ti multi-mount winch. He installed a second Optima yellow top battery in the back. Using quick-connect plugs, it can be wired in a series with the front battery providing 24 volts for the Ready Welder that he also carries. John has also recently fabricated a set of half doors.

By this time, *The Badger* was a very capable rock crawler, but John wasn't done yet! The Rusty's long-arm suspension in the front out-flexed the rear leaf springs by a mile, so John's goal was to balance the suspension. He used a custom four-link coil-over suspension that worked out perfectly. Details of his coil-over project are featured earlier in Chapter 2. ∎

The evolution of John's XJ includes a rear coil-over suspension with RaceRunner shocks from Sway-A-Way. This photo also shows the newly added hydraulic bumpstops. (Photo Courtesy John Laurella)

The long-arm suspension gives the front axle insane amounts of droop. Along with front and rear lockers, this is a very capable rock crawler. (Photo Courtesy John Laurella)

The custom brack-etry on the front axle is very impressive. This is the raised track bar mount that matches the geometry of the over-the-knuckle steering. (Photo Courtesy John Laurella)

The rear coil-overs complement the front long-arms nicely, giving The Badger a balanced suspension that produces extreme amounts of flex. (Photo Courtesy John Laurella)

BODY BASICS

If you've read the book up to this point, you probably already know that the Cherokee is a unibody, as opposed to a vehicle with a body on a frame. The Cherokee does get a bad rap now and then for being a unibody, which does have its disadvantages. But let's not forget history. The Cherokee's unibody construction played a big part in its claim to fame in the mid-1980s. Why don't you see many full-size Wagoneers out on the trails? The main reason is size and weight. Because of the unibody construction, the Cherokee is smaller and substantially lighter than its predecessors. So, is the unibody preferred over a solid frame for off-road use? No, certainly not. Off-road is where the unibody takes the most punishment and shows its weaknesses. But if it weren't for the unibody construction, the Cherokee would not have been nearly as successful as it was. This chapter gives a general overview of the body and offers some suggestions on how to strengthen it.

Two-Door versus Four-Door

The Cherokee came in both two-door and four-door models. So which is better and why? Many peo-

This is the underside of an XJ showing where the frame rail is attached to the body. XJs are unibody vehicles that do not have a traditional body-on-frame design, so the body cannot be separated from the frame.

ple like the two-door, even if it's just for looks. That's great for some people, and nobody can tell you what to like. I could go on about how the passenger doors are more convenient but that's just my opinion, too. However, from a structural standpoint, the four-door is better for a couple of reasons.

The overall dimensions of the two-door and four-door bodies are

the same. The difference, other than the obvious number of doors, is the size of the doors and the number of pillars in the body. The doors of a two-door XJ are quite a bit larger than the front doors of a four-door. That makes them very heavy. Over time, the hinges may suffer due to the weight. The hinges are welded to the body, so replacement is not

Four-door XJs have four pillars, illustrated by the A, B, C, and D above. Two-door XJs only have three pillars: the A-pillar, the rearmost pillar, and a pillar in the middle.

A few creative XJ owners have built their own half-doors. Most guys who have half-doors use a spare set of doors that they can put on or take off as needed. That way they still have their original doors, too. (Photo Courtesy John Laurella)

easy. The stress on the door hinges is unlikely to affect the overall strength of the vehicle, but the number of pillars is more important to consider.

Four-door XJs have four pillars, named A, B, C, and D. The A-pillar is the front pillar (where the front door hinges are) that makes up the sides of the windshield. The B-pillar is between the front and rear passenger doors. The C-pillar is behind the rear passenger door, and the D-pillar is at the rear of the vehicle. The two-door XJ only has three pillars. The A-pillar is the same as on the four-door. The B-pillar is in the center of the vehicle. And the C-pillar is at the rear. Having the extra pillar on the four-door models is sure to add more strength to the body as a whole. By no means does this suggest that the two-door XJ is inferior or unsuitable for extreme use off-road. A lot of that depends on your driving style and what you do to strengthen and stiffen the body. Both two-door and four-door XJs can use some unibody stiffening.

The doors themselves do not add to the strength of the body. Because of this, many people modify the hinge so that the doors can be removed for off-road use. This is a great way to shed some weight for the trail, but be prepared to weather the elements if you do.

Some people also like to get a spare set of doors and make half-doors out of them. The window glass and regulators are gutted out and then the shape of the half-doors can be cut. The inside panel is re-skinned and finished to your liking. On the trail, everyone seems to drive with their head out of the window to try to get a better view of the terrain. That's a whole lot easier with half doors.

The rear hatch, or lift gate, is also a door, and it is available in two

Half-doors make trail riding that much more fun and increase visibility. Be careful you don't fall out, John!

This is a cracked fiberglass hatch on a 1995 XJ. Nick, the owner, came down very hard on a big rock and the body flexed, causing his strong Tomken rear bumper to contact the hatch. The opposite corner also cracked in the same place. He thought he only lost part of a taillight until he got out and saw this!

versions. The fiberglass hatches came in 1984–1996 XJs. These are weak and have been known to break on the trail, sometimes spitting out the rear window glass. Along with the newer body upgrades in 1997, the rear hatch was changed to metal to match the rest of the body. These hatches are much stronger than the fiberglass hatches, so they don't start to fall apart on you. Changing from a fiberglass hatch to a metal one would be nice, but it's not an easy task. The hinges of the fiberglass hatches are on the outside, on the roof. The hinges for the metal hatches are on the inside, on the back face of the header panel, so it will take some custom work to make it happen.

Unibody Strengthening and Stiffening

More than likely, the first time you noticed how much the body flexes was when you were off-road; you saw a big rock and thought it would be cool to test the suspension. So you max the suspension travel and start to open the door to get out and take a look. The door pops open and makes an unusual sound. It feels like there was a load on the latch. When you get back in and shut the door, it sounds and feels like it's misaligned, but it still shuts; at least you hope it does! If your body flexes when you get all twisted up on the trail and the door doesn't close, you should definitely consider some ways to strengthen and stiffen up the unibody. When you get the Jeep back on level ground, the doors usually operate the same as they did before. The unibody just flexed some, putting stress on the latch. This is relatively harmless, and it happens to all XJs. But over time it may become worse, depending on how hard you are on the Jeep and how frequently you like to get twisted up in gnarly terrain.

What about sunroofs? They can pose a problem also. A sunroof doesn't necessarily make the unibody any weaker, but on an off-road rig that likes to flex, the seal around the sunroof might be compromised, causing the sunroof to develop leaks when it rains.

Crossmembers

Even though there isn't a real frame under the XJ, it does have two frame rails that run the length of the vehicle. The metal of the XJ frame

The T&T Customs belly pan is one of the best crossmembers since it attaches to both frame rails with at least 10 bolts, 6 of which sleeve the frame rails. If you get just the belly pan without the long-arms, fewer bolts mount it, but either way, it will help stiffen the unibody quite a bit.

This Rubicon Express track-bar brace helps stiffen up the front end. The brace only lined up with one of the holes on the passenger-side frame rail. (Maybe I flexed the Jeep one too many times before I got it!) I made a plate for the bolts to go through that sandwiches that part of the frame rail, so it's secured by three bolts now, instead of two.

Above and below: This is the C-ROK exo-cage for the two-door XJ. It is designed to work best with C-ROK bumpers and rocker guards, but is modified easily to work with any aftermarket bumpers. Notice how it clamps to the drip rail of the roof in six locations. (Photo Courtesy C-ROK Engineering and Fabrication)

rails is very thin, but at least it's thicker than other body panels and sheet metal. The frame is meant to be the most rigid part of the structure. Some solid-framed vehicles have a ladder frame with supports or cross-members that connect the two frame rails. Like a ladder, the more rungs or steps a ladder has, the less it twists. The same is true for the XJ. The XJ has one crossmember centered under the body to support the transmission and transfer case. There are two more crossmembers, one at the front of the vehicle, sometimes called the "bulkhead," and one at the rear. So how can you add more crossmembers?

For this discussion, I'm defining a "crossmember" as any rigid, fixed object that connects the frame rails. Solid front or rear bumpers qualify as crossmembers. A strong aftermarket front bumper can stiffen up the front end considerably. The same goes for

Mike Hobbs did a great job on his own tube fenders. These are not just for looks! This is the beginning stage of a cage that will tie everything together.

the rear. A front receiver hitch could also act as a crossmember. One very good crossmember is a track-bar brace. This brace connects to the track bar mount on the driver's side, fits under the oil pan, and connects to the passenger-side frame rail. Its primary purpose is to give support to the track bar mount, which tends to come loose. Heck, even a steering-box brace might qualify as a crossmember. Aftermarket transfer-case skids that span both frame rails help, as do some gas-tank skids. For the rear,

some people fabricate a shock hoop as an alternate place to mount the shocks. If done correctly, this could add some structural integrity as well.

Stiffeners

HD Offroad, Ruff Stuff Specialties, Detours Offroad, T&J Performance, and T&T Customs offer frame rail stiffeners that are welded along the frame rail and attach to the rear leaf-spring mount and the front control-arm mount. These stiffeners are designed to make the frame rails more rigid. A good set of rock rails can have a similar benefit, depending on how many places along the frame rail it attaches and whether or not it bolts to the pinch seam underneath. Some guys reinforce the frame rails with 3/16-inch scrap steel or angle iron. This adds a lot of weight to the vehicle, but it adds considerable strength and stiffness to the unibody. Kind of like having a real frame!

Cages

Exo-cages and regular interior cages are a great way to strengthen

the whole unibody structure. A bad rollover is often a death sentence for the unibody. Cages are meant to keep the unibody straight and protect the driver and passengers. Good exo-cages tie everything together: the front bumpers, the rock rails, and the rear bumper. A "halo" over the roof offers good protection and can double as a roof rack. Some guys are coming up with some pretty ingenious designs, such as going through the roof and tying it all together with an inner cage.

T&J Performance and D&C Extreme are two companies that make pre-fabbed weld-in cage kits; a bolt-in kit is available from Rock Hard 4x4. Any of these kits provide some protection during a rollover. However, sometimes it is better to have a custom cage built by a competent fabricator.

Fender Trimming

One of the most frequently asked questions is, "How big a tire can I fit without trimming?" If you

This is the second round of trimming on Project Rubicon, *this time to fit 35s. The front is easy to trim; just tape off the fender to mark where you want to cut (which also protects the body from being scratched). I used a jigsaw with a very fine-toothed blade to make this cut.*

You can trim the rear fenders the same way as the front; just don't cut past the spot welds. This shows about how far up you can trim before the inner and outer fenders separate.

To open up the fender even more, make some small relief cuts and bend the flaps back up into the fender. Doing it this way keeps the spot welds intact so the fender pieces don't separate.

Here is the finished rear fender. The paint will flake along the edge from the metal being bent back, but it can be covered with paint or bed liner.

ask this, I can assume that you aren't building this for off-road use, right? Anything larger than a 31-inch tire does not physically fit in a fender-well with untrimmed fenders when the suspension flexes. Even 31s rub, depending on the backspacing. Sometimes it's just a matter of removing the stock front bumper end caps. Or you may just need to remove the flares if they keep getting pushed off. But for anything bigger than a 31-inch tire on an XJ built for off-road, you need to break out that Sawzall, cutting wheel, jigsaw, or cutting tool of your choice.

The front fenders are easy. Just tape off where you want to trim and trim away. I found that a jigsaw with a very fine-toothed blade (at least 24 tpi) works well. For the rear fenders, you need to pay attention to the spot welds that connect the inner fender and outer fenders. Don't cut past those spot welds or you'll need to re-weld the fenders together. A good method for the rear is to cut some small relief cuts into the fender where the bends in the opening are, and then hammer to

bend up the part of the fender you want to remove. Use silicone sealant to seal the bent-up sections of fender and prevent them from rusting. Be prepared to paint over the edges that you bent because the factory paint will be flaking in those areas.

The rear quarter panels are an extremely vulnerable spot on the XJ.

Along with trimming the fenders, some people like to cut and fold up the lower sections of the rear quarters. When done right, this modification can look great as well as help your departure angle. Some guys leave the area open, and others make custom bumpers that wrap around the corner for protection.

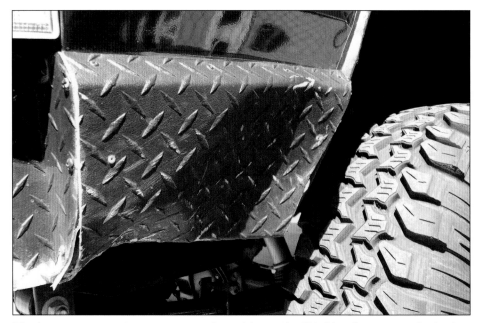

The lower rear quarters are very vulnerable on the XJ. Aluminum guards don't provide much strength, as you can see. Several companies sell steel guards that provide better protection.

On this XJ, the lower quarters were cut and folded up, creating a lot of clearance. It can be left open like this, or protected with a custom bumper that wraps around the corner.

After the panels were cut and folded up, they were re-welded to the body.

Flare Options

After the fenders are trimmed, you need to decide what to do about the fender flares. In my state, I'm lucky because the officials don't care whether you have flares at all. Other states like to see your tires covered.

There are a lot of flare options, including relocating the stock flares higher, using flares from another vehicle (TJ flares and MJ flares are good ones), or purchasing aftermarket flares such as those from BushWacker or Napier Precision Products. Bush-Wackers probably give you the most coverage, since they are extremely wide. They're so wide, in fact, that they can make your big tires look small. But you can't beat the protection they give to the body. It seems that people either love the way they look, or hate them. All I'll say here is that I've seen some pretty bad hack jobs, and a good set of flares such as BushWackers can help cover up any goofs you make.

When *Project Rubicon* was on 33s, I trimmed the flares and relocated them higher: only a slight amount in the rear (about 3/8 inch) and about 1 inch in the front. I did like the look, but the stock retaining brackets are very difficult to work with, and at first I had problems keeping some of the flares attached. After a few tries I got it right, but it was a big hassle. Now I'm running flareless, and I'm glad I don't have to worry about my flares falling off. The bad thing is that the sides of the Jeep get a lot dirtier. Hey, I'll admit that I like my Jeep looking good between trail runs!

These are BushWacker cut-out flares covering a 33 x 12.50–inch tire. The wheel used here has 4.5 inches of backspacing, so it's tucked in quite a bit.

One half of the rear BushWacker flare mounts onto the rear door on the four-door model. Flares for two-door XJs are also available.

These are rear flares from an MJ Comanche. The MJ flares are longer than XJ flares, so they are ideal to use after you trim the fenders. Bryan Vetrano cut them in half to mount one side onto the door.

With the door shut, you can see how these flares look like they were put there from the factory. The style of the flare matches Bryan's front XJ flare exactly.

*This is **Project Rubicon** with the stock flares relocated higher up. The lower portions of the flares were cut off to give them more of an even look and eliminate the gap created when they were moved up.*

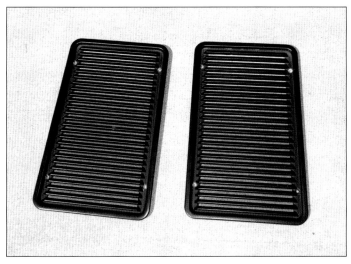

These are hood vents from a 1980s Chrysler LeBaron Turbo or New Yorker. I pulled them from the junkyard for about $12.

The size of the vents are just right to miss the hood supports. Some XJ hoods have slightly different supports, but to my knowledge the vents will fit no matter what year XJ you have.

This is what it looks like with two big holes in your hood. The driver-side opening is directly over the exhaust and intake manifolds, which is an ideal location for a vent. You'll notice more heat rising from this side than from the passenger's side.

The vents can be secured with small sections of angled aluminum to clamp them to the hood. A strip of angled aluminum can be found at most hardware stores.

Hood Vents

In 2003, I decided to hack two big holes in my Jeep's perfect hood to add some hood vents. I had seen a few people do it before, but there weren't really any good "how-to" write-ups that I could find on the subject. I ended up putting my own hood-vent write-up online, and it has generated a lot of interest. Lately, it seems as though everyone is doing it,

at least all of the XJs in my local club, and that's not a bad thing. My vents are due for a touch-up paint job, so this book was the perfect opportunity to remove the vents and walk you through the installation as best I can with some new photos.

For starters, let me explain why I, or anyone else, would want to install some hood vents. Believe it or not, I have actually had a few people ask me if those vents are real, meaning

that they actually let out heat. The normal operating temperature for the 4.0L engine is around 210 degrees on the highway. On a hot, dusty trail, or in stop-and-go city traffic, it's not unusual to see the temperatures climb up into the 225-degree range or higher, due to poor airflow through the radiator. This is normal, too, because per the factory service manual, the auxiliary fan turns on when the coolant temperature rises to 223

I think these vents look almost factory on the XJ. The square style matches the lines of the boxy XJ.

degrees F regardless of whether or not you have the air conditioning on. The auxiliary fan remains on until the temperature drops to 217 degrees F. On the trail, out in the middle of nowhere, I didn't like worrying about the engine temperatures, and hearing the auxiliary fan on all the time adding to my anxiety.

These hood vents are from a 1980s Chrysler LeBaron Turbo, but they can also be found on some Chrysler New Yorkers. They are made of thick fiberglass, and when I first felt how heavy they were, I thought they might be cast out of metal. They also have a pretty large surface area compared to other vents. I think they look like they were meant to be on a Jeep Cherokee. Here are ten tips to help you through the install:

1. First things first: Clean up the vents and give them a fresh coat of paint.

2. Decide if you want to do this modification with the hood attached to the vehicle or removed from the vehicle (either is okay).

3. Using masking tape, tape off the area where the vents will go. You really don't have much of a choice; they need to go between the hood supports on the underside of the hood.

4. If your hood has the hood insulation, remove it.

5. Carefully measure and mark on the tape where you will cut, taking care to have the vents centered and evenly spaced from the centerline of the hood. Take measurements from under the hood to avoid cutting into the hood supports (it's okay if you cut into them slightly).

6. Recheck your measurements. You only get one chance to get it right.

7. If the hood is still on the vehicle, cover the windshield, engine, and other areas of the hood that may become scratched during the cutting.

8. Cut the hood. I used an angle grinder with cut-off wheel, and it ended up flaking off some paint around the cuts. A jigsaw with a very fine-toothed blade would have been a better choice.

9. Remove the tape and clean up the edges of the cut for a perfect fit.

10. Secure the vents using small angled pieces of aluminum or thin-gauged steel that will clamp the vents to the underside of the hood when bolted down.

After installing the vents, I noticed the temp gauge stayed an honest 5 to 10 degrees lower on the trail. The auxiliary fan still turns on, but not as often as before. There is no noticeable decrease in temperature on the highway, since the airflow through the radiator is already sufficient. These vents are not designed to act as a scoop or to produce a lot of airflow through them. They work best at slow speeds or when the vehicle is stopped and idling. Even after the engine is turned off, you can see heat continue to billow out of the vents. It is pretty neat to do a modification when you can see the results on a gauge, but even more so when you can see it with your own eyes. Even if your temp gauge doesn't work, there would be no doubt in your mind that these vents release copious amounts of heat from the engine compartment.

Bedlining the Interior

Because I flooded my interior on the Rubicon Trail, I had the

You can bet the owner of this Jeep wasn't too pleased when he discovered this rust under the carpet in the cargo area. It is so bad that it has eaten a hole through the metal.

The same XJ had even more rust under the rear seat area. Rusted areas in key locations such as where side panels meet the floor can affect the strength of your unibody. In the long run, early detection and repair will be worth every penny.

interior completely stripped out to let the carpet and seats dry. I took this opportunity to add some protection so that in the future I won't need to worry about rust developing from the inside of the Jeep. Rust does happen, especially if you have any leaks in the roof or doors that get the carpet wet. Underneath the carpet is a pad similar to the pad under your carpet at home. This pad can soak up a lot of water and take months, if not longer, to dry inside the vehicle.

I also added a few more drain holes because I didn't feel that the stock ones were adequate. The stock holes in my XJ were located behind the driver's and passenger's front seats, and there were four in the rear cargo area, two of which were totally useless. I patched the two useless drain holes and used those two rubber plugs for the drain holes I'd be adding. I added a drain hole in the floorboards of both driver's and front passenger's foot areas, but in the most out-of-the-way locations. I also added two 1/2-inch drain holes in the storage compartment under the rear bench seat. I used 1/2-inch "bailer plugs" that I found at Wal-Mart to plug these holes. These were strategic locations where I witnessed water collecting after my underwater excursion!

I chose Herculiner bed liner to coat the interior. The interior surface needs to be prepped first, and the worst part of the job was removing the sound-deadener pads that were there from the factory. All surfaces

The one-gallon Herculiner kit was the perfect amount to do the entire floor of the XJ with two coats. This kit was purchased at AutoZone for a little under $100. You need to buy the Xylene and paint pan separately.

This is the interior with everything stripped out and prepped for the Herculiner. Thankfully, having a newer XJ in a dry climate, rust is not that much of a problem.

This is one of the new drain holes I added. I chose this location because it is a lower part of the floor and not usually where I rest my feet. I added one in this spot on the passenger's side as well.

I am very pleased with how the Herculiner project turned out. The strength and adhesiveness of the Herculiner was impressive. It can be left as is or you can put the carpet back in.

need to be cleaned thoroughly for the bed liner to be effective. You can scuff the surface with the Scotch pad included in the kit, or use sandpaper if necessary. Then clean the surface again using xylene (Xylol) or acetone. Wear gloves when using these chemicals, and make sure there's good ventilation (all doors open) and no heat sources or open flames nearby. Apply two coats of Herculiner, again wearing gloves. I didn't for the first coat, and my hands stayed black for days. One gallon of Herculiner was perfect for two coats, and I am very pleased with the results. The bed liner is much stronger than I thought it would be. I replaced the carpet but removed the pad from underneath. I also cut the carpet into smaller sections that can be removed like floor mats without having to take out the seats or remove any trim panels.

SKID PLATES AND RECOVERY

Even though this is the last chapter of the book, don't wait until the end of your build-up to add protection to your Jeep! Some of these items should be added first, maybe even before the lift kit, and preferably before you venture out on a trail that might challenge your stock XJ or your driving skills. You want to make sure that you and your passengers can get home safely.

When I purchased my 2000 XJ new from the dealership, it had no skid plates and no tow hooks. Although these items were more standard with the older XJs, I think Jeep realized that the majority of Cherokee owners were never going to really go off-road. Therefore, tow hooks and skid plates had to be ordered as an option. That's okay, though, because you want something strong that's going to protect the Jeep no matter what; and sometimes the stock stuff just isn't up to that task.

Front Recovery Points

If you get stuck and need to be strapped or winched, where will you attach the strap? It's not a good idea to wrap the strap around the axle, or the stock bumper. You need a strong

Dustin Mills has a winch on his custom-built front bumper. Winches are great for recovery, but they can be very heavy. This tube frame bumper is lightweight, which helps offset the weight of the winch.

recovery point that you are confident will hold and not cause damage or injury in a recovery attempt.

Tow hooks work, but they're not the best option. If you choose to install tow hooks, you must buy tow-hook brackets along with the hooks themselves. The frame rails are too thin to support just the hook, and you don't want that hook getting ripped out, which can happen. And don't even think of bolting the

tow hooks straight onto the stock bumper! Most aftermarket tow-hook brackets for XJs attach to the three stock bumper mounting holes and also tie into the big hole that is about 8 inches farther back on the frame rail. The disadvantage of using tow hooks is that they are not as strong when being pulled from the side or at an angle.

A front receiver hitch also works as a front recovery point, but the

The front bumper on Mike Hobb's XJ is built by Rigidco. It features an integrated 2-inch receiver, 1-inch-thick shackle tabs, the optional pre-runner bar, and an excellent mounting system that ties into the frame rails and front bulkhead, and reinforces the steering box.

These are Rusty's tow hook brackets. A tow hook bracket is absolutely necessary when mounting tow hooks to an XJ. Notice that the bracket mounts in the same location as the bumper bracket, but it also has a mounting point farther back on the frame rail.

A 2-inch front receiver hitch makes for a good recovery point. It will give up some clearance, but that's better than not having a recovery point.

best option is an aftermarket bumper with tow loops, an integrated hitch, or a mount for a winch. When choosing a front bumper, look for one that ties into the frame rails in more places than just the stock bumper mounts. Weak bumpers can be ripped off your XJ. A strong front bumper can also be used as a jacking point.

Rear Recovery Points

For the rear, the same rule applies for tow hooks. They must be supported with some sort of bracket. Rear tow hooks are less common, and most people prefer to use a 2-inch receiver hitch instead. The only bad thing about receiver hitches is that you give up some clearance, which can be an issue, as XJs aren't known for having a good departure angle to begin with. Again, an aftermarket or custom bumper with tow loops or an integrated receiver is usually the best option. Look for a rear bumper with mounts that tie into the frame rails and not just to the body alone. A heavy-duty rear bumper can also serve as a good jacking point on the trail.

The following is a list of manufacturers that make bumpers for the Cherokee. Many of these companies also offer rear tire carriers, rock rails, and a wide variety of skid plates. (See the Source Guide on page 143 for contact information.)

This is a stock rear tow hook. Notice that it also uses an additional bracket that attaches to the stock bumper and the frame rail. Even with that bracket, it isn't a reliable recovery point, because pulling from an angle will likely bend it.

- AJ's Offroad Armor
- ARB 4x4 Accessories
- C-ROK Engineering and Fabrication
- Custom 4x4 Fabrication
- Detours Manufacturing
- DPG Off-Road
- Hanson Offroad
- JCR Offroad
- Olympic 4x4 Products

Project Rubicon gets to free a stuck Grand Cherokee. The AEV rear bumper has tow loops that tie directly into the frame-rail mounts. The Grand has an ARB winch bumper with no winch yet, so we used the tow loops that are also included on that bumper.

- OR-Fab
- Proto Fab
- Rigid Fabrication and Manufacturing
- Rock Hard 4x4
- Rusty's Off-Road Products
- Skid Row Automotive
- Smittybilt
- Tomken
- TrailReady
- Warn Industries
- Warrior Products

Transfer Case Protection

The transfer case is a vital driveline component, and being located right in the middle of the Jeep makes it vulnerable in situations where you might become high centered. The stock transfer-case skid offers poor protection, but it is better than nothing. Luckily, several aftermarket skids are available that offer much better protection than the stock skid. Adding a heavy-duty transfer-case skid can protect your transfer case from damage and give you something to slide on as you pass over obstacles. The skid needs to be able to support most of the vehicle's weight without bending; there will no doubt be times when you end up resting on the skid on top of an obstacle.

Gas Tank Protection

The gas tank is also vulnerable in many situations. Older XJs had metal tanks, which were "upgraded" to plastic in the newer models. Whether you have a plastic or metal tank, consider yourself lucky if you hit it and all it does is become dented, reducing its capacity. Worst-case scenario, it ruptures and your gas spills out on the trail. Unlike the transfer-case skid, the stock skid for the gas tank is a fairly decent unit. If you have one, keep it. If you don't, buy an aftermarket one or look for a stock tank at the junkyard. On more than one

Here is a stock transfer-case skid. It is not very strong, but it's better than nothing.

This is Travis Thompson's indestructible crossmember and stock transfer-case skid (that also has been reinforced).

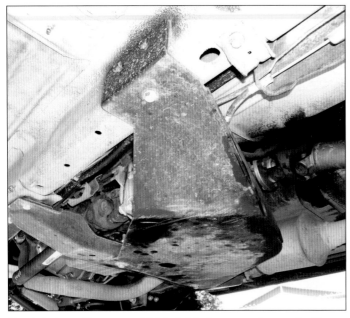

Rusty's transfer-case skid is fairly inexpensive and offers pretty good protection. It is made of 3/16-inch steel and is gusseted in the back for rigidity.

The T&T Custom's belly pan offers mounting points for the long-arm suspension, and also doubles as a strong transfer-case skid. The pan is made of 1/4-inch steel and extends forward 6 inches from the original crossmember location to offer some protection to the transmission pan.

The Tomken gas-tank skid offers fair protection. Even though it's only 1/8-inch steel, it is boxed on all sides, which adds to the strength. It has saved my butt a few times. Also notice the differential guard on the rear axle.

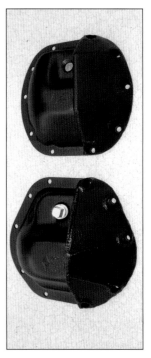

Barnett HD differential covers are sold by T&J Performance. These differential covers, as well as most other styles of rock rings and differential guards, help strengthen the differential housing as a whole.

Differential Guards

occasion, I have seen a gas tank skid just laying next to the XJ at the junkyard. Apparently the people who came before were after the gas tank itself and just left the skid there for easy pickings. Be aware that for the skid plate to bolt up to the frame rail, you may need to grab the nut strip, or "sill reinforcement" strip, that slides into the frame rail.

These can be worth their weight in gold if you play in the rocks. A smashed differential cover can take out your ring and pinion, which isn't pretty. Not only can a differential

These control-arm mounts have been plated with JKS "miniskids." The rock rash on them is evidence that they are well used and worth having.

guard prevent that from happening, but it can also strengthen your differential housing. Of course, the front differential is more vulnerable than the rear, but I've hit my rear differential guard much more than I ever thought I would. It's definitely worth every dime I spent on it. Some differential guards are beefed-up replacement covers. Others are like a football helmet face mask that bolts on over the stock cover using longer differential-cover bolts.

Control-Arm Protection

You can beef up your control-arm mounts by adding a plate to the front of the control-arm mount. This protects the front of the control arm from rocks in the same way that differential guards protect the differential. Most control arms are able to take some rock abuse, but the mounts themselves are not that strong and can be ripped from the axle tube. Welding on a plate

as a control-arm skid adds a lot of strength to the mounts.

Rocker Panel Protection

Minor rocker panel dents could be considered cosmetic. Bigger dents could mean that you'll be exiting the XJ through the window because the door no longer opens. If you don't feel like doing the Dukes of Hazzard thing every time you get in and out, or you just want to keep your rockers looking nice, you need a strong set of rock rails. Older versions of these were the "nerf bars" that you see a lot on Toyota trucks. Steer far away from this design, as it is more for looks than protection. The same thing goes for running boards; they are junk when it comes to protecting the sides of your Jeep. Unfortunately, many aftermarket rock-rails are marginal at best, and still bends up into your rocker panels with serious use. Here are some features to look for when choosing a set of rock rails:

- They stick out from the sides of the Jeep. This makes them handy as a step, but also adds more side protection to the body. It also helps for pivoting around big rocks.

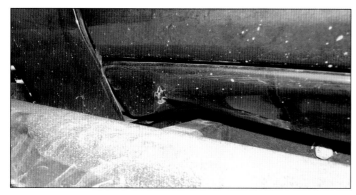

I hate to say it, but most rock rails on the market will flex up into your rockers with serious use. These are the Rocky Road Outfitter (RRO) step rails. All four corners of the rockers look similar to this.

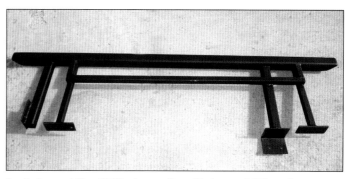

I reinforced the RRO step rails with two additional mounting arms on each rail. These arms tie into the side and bottom of the frame rail and the front leaf-spring mount. I have had no problems with the rails bending up after correcting RRO's poor design.

Tom Moser cut out his rockers and welded in a 2 x 4–inch length of 3/16-inch-thick steel. Then he added round tubing for added side protection. We found that these replacement rockers still need to be tied into the frame rails. Otherwise, you can still bend the body if you come down really hard on them.

Steve's Zebra XJ has its spare tire on the roof rack. The rack also holds his off-road lights and Hi-Lift jack. Note the custom-built exo-cage.

- They mount to the sides of the frame rail as well as to the bottom (this may interfere with some items such as control-arm drop brackets) and/or:
- They attach to the front leaf-spring mounts.
- They attach along the pinch seam (this may not be ultimately necessary depending on the design of the other mounts).
- They are made of at least 3/16-inch steel.

Another nice benefit of rock rails is that they can be used as a jacking point for the Hi-Lift jack. Cutting out the rocker panels and welding in a 2 x 4–inch or 2 x 6–inch rail of 3/16-inch steel is another option. Be sure to also tie them into the frame rails because the body can still bend if you come down hard on them.

Spare Tire Location

Every trail rig needs a full-size spare tire, but a big tire doesn't fit in the stock location. For some people this is a dilemma of magnificent proportions, because they can't decide where to store it. Here are the most common options for mounting a spare tire. I'll let you decide which is best for you.

Keep It Inside

Probably the cheapest way to store the spare is to keep it inside the Jeep. For big tires, such as 35s, that means laying it flat in the back with the back seat down or removed. The bad thing about this is the loss of interior cargo space and seating. Even though it's inside the Jeep, make sure that it is securely tied down so it doesn't fly around in the event of a rollover or accident.

This is Bryan Vetrano's custom rear bumper and tire carrier. He included mounts for his Hi-Lift jack on the carrier.

Here is Lee Harper's Jeep (left) parked next to mine (right). Lee has Custom 4x4 Fabrication's rear bumper and tire carrier, which is popular and reasonably priced. The AEV bumper and tire carrier I have was expensive and is out of production.

larger tires on the roof with room for other items as well.

As you might imagine, there are a few disadvantages to having it up there. A full-size spare can weigh 75 pounds or more, so getting it up and down is sure to be a chore. That weight also raises the vehicle's center of gravity, and the tire also likely creates wind drag, resulting in a loss of fuel efficiency on the highway.

On the Back

Some XJs actually came with rear tire carriers, which can accommodate up to a 31-inch tire. If you don't have the stock carrier, or you're using larger than a 31-inch spare, an aftermarket tire carrier can be purchased to go along with an aftermarket rear bumper, but they are not cheap. I have seen many well-built custom carriers that look just as good as any other tire carrier on the market. Like putting the spare on the roof, the big benefit of a tire carrier is getting it out of the interior, which frees up space. However, with the tire on the back, it's easier to access and doesn't raise the vehicle's center of gravity as much. They look pretty good on the back, too!

There is even another less obvious benefit from having the spare on the back. Because the XJ is shaped like a brick, a lot of dirt collects on the rear window due to a void created when the air passes over the top of the Jeep. That's why they sell those rear air deflectors: to improve airflow, which eliminates this void. Well, with the rear tire carrier, the tire fills this void, and I have noticed that the rear window stays much cleaner than before.

The main disadvantage of rear tire carriers is the high price tag. Some people also consider the tire

On the Top

Keeping the spare up on the roof is another very popular option. Not only does it free up space in the interior, but I have to admit that I love the look of a meaty tire up on the roof.

The Mopar tire carrier that attaches to the stock roof rack might be strong enough for a small tire such as a 31. The better way would be to install an aftermarket roof rack. These are strong enough to accommodate even blocking the rear window as a disadvantage, but after a while you get used to using the side mirrors. At least the guy behind you with his brights on won't be as annoying anymore! One other disadvantage is that the tire can reduce the departure angle somewhat. On more than one occasion, I have come down off a ledge, or begun to climb a steep obstacle, and had the tire on the back hit the ledge or drag on the ground. As a result, I keep that tire aired down a fair amount to help the tire absorb any hits it may take. So far the tire dragging hasn't been a serious issue for me, but if the tire was any lower on the bumper, it could be more of a problem. So, when choosing a rear tire carrier, the height of the tire on the back is something to consider as well.

Basic Tools for Recovery

Off-road driving can be fun and exciting, but there are risks associated with this sport. People have been seriously injured or killed by not being prepared and not having the right tools for the job.

Tow Straps

One of the number-one recovery no-nos is using straps with hooks. Hooks on straps can break, and when they do, they fly at bullet-fast speeds. You can imagine what happens to those who have been hit by one, so I won't demonstrate that procedure for you! So, buy tow straps with loops, and not hooks.

Two-inch-wide tow straps with a 20,000-pound rating are strong enough for most pulls. If you have broken a 2-inch-wide tow strap, then you may want to upgrade to a 3-inch-wide 30,000-pound strap. I carry two 2-inch-wide straps that

Basic recovery tools and equipment, like a Hi-Lift, four-way, shovel, etc. are a must. Go prepared and be safe!

are 20 feet long, and I've used them several times without breaking one. But I must confess, I also have a 3-inch-wide strap for backup. Who wants to get stuck or stranded?

Winches

A winch is the ultimate recovery tool. Although wheeling by yourself isn't recommended, a winch allows you to extract your Jeep if you get stuck. They are also much better than tow straps in a variety of situations such as righting a rolled vehicle. Winches are most often mounted to an aftermarket winch bumper, but another option is to use a winch cradle that slides into a 2-inch receiver. As with any other heavy item you carry, make sure it is strapped down inside the Jeep when not in use. Regardless of which brand of winch you buy, it must be able to pull twice the weight of your Jeep. Because most Cherokees weigh roughly 4,000 pounds, make sure your winch has an 8,000-pound or greater pull rating. A hand-winch or come-along are alternatives to winches. A Hi-Lift jack can also be used as a come-along if you have straps and a length of strong chain.

Jacks

Hi-Lift jacks are great, but they can be dangerous if not used properly. Make sure you read the instructions prior to use and keep the pins lubricated for trouble-free operation.

You should also have rock rails or heavy-duty aftermarket bumpers that you can use as jacking points. Why use a Hi-Lift jack if you don't have any jacking points? Sometimes a Hi-Lift jack is impractical for changing a tire because with the sway bars disconnected you need to jack the body up extremely high before the tire comes off the ground. For this reason, using a small bottle jack under an axle is much easier. That way, you lift the vehicle up as little as necessary to change a tire. It is wise to carry both a small bottle jack and a Hi-Lift jack, since one may work better than the other depending on the situation.

Spares

Now think about your vehicle. What spare parts should you take? The answer is largely determined by how far you go, what the terrain is like, the condition of your Jeep before you go, etc. For difficult trails, spare axle shafts are a good idea. Also take

Rock rails and heavy-duty bumpers make good jacking points for the Hi-Lift jack. Be warned: You will bend your stock bumpers and unprotected rocker panels if you use them as a jacking point.

about toilet paper? Ah, yes. . . the necessities! If you're used to the outdoors and camping, this may be second nature to you. Maybe my few words in this section will help somebody by getting them to think about these things.

If you are going on a day trip, prepare as if you are spending the night. You don't need a tent, grill, and all that, but definitely pack some extra food, water, warm clothes, and yes, toilet paper. If you are going for an overnighter, take enough to get by for two nights if you had to, etc. One easy way to do this is to put together a "ready bag" of stuff you would need. Keep it packed and ready to go; that way you can just throw it into the Jeep and take it out when you are done. You don't need to re-pack it every time.

It's also a good idea not to go Jeeping alone. Go with friends: If one vehicle breaks down, at least you have a ride out.

a spare tie-rod if you haven't beefed up your steering already. Don't forget some fluids, including gear oil and ATF, and don't forget that tube of RTV. Think about what is most likely to break and prepare for that. Don't go overboard and bring one of everything; your rig won't be able to carry all that weight!

Tools

Make sure you have at least some basic tools with you. I have been out on a trail when someone needed to change a tire but had no tools, not even a lug wrench. They did have a spare tire, though! You don't need overkill on the tools, either. Many times, duct tape and baling wire work well in a pinch, but I would feel pretty helpless if that's all I had to work with.

Survival Tips

Think about what accidents might happen, and ask yourself what

you would do in that situation. Do you have a fire extinguisher? First-aid kit? An extra jacket or blanket? How

John Laurella carries the following in the back of his XJ: multi-mount winch, 4 gallons of water, 6 quarts of oil, 2 quarts of gear lube, an extra air filter, a tree strap, a 6-foot choker chain, four D-ring shackles, a snatch block, a full tool box, a jumper pack, and a Ready Welder. He also has a Hi-Lift jack and shovel stored on his roof rack. (Photo Courtesy John Laurella)

Jeep XJ Profile: The Reno 4x4 XJs Do the Rubicon

This is the XJ group ready to start the trail. From left to right: me, Tom, Travis, John, and Dustin. You don't need the biggest XJ to handle the Rubicon. The right combination of modifications and driver skill will get you through.

After a long winter, some of the XJ guys from our local group (including myself) were off to do the long-awaited Rubicon Trail run. Even though it was late June, there was still snow, but the trail reports from a few weeks prior were that the snow on the 'Con was melting fast and groups were making it through to Tahoe. Not only were we anxious to do some wheeling away from home, but we also knew the Rubicon would be a good test for our rigs, all of which got a little bigger and badder over the winter.

There were five XJs that headed up on Sunday afternoon: myself and my son Taylor; Tom and his son Hayden; Dustin; Travis; and John. Our XJs were well equipped: *Project Rubicon* and Dustin's rig both had 4.56:1s, front and rear lockers, and 35s. Tom, Travis, and John's XJs all had between

Tom gets high-centered on Gatekeeper. I gave him a tug with a tow strap to get him off this rock. Unfortunately, the forest service later dynamited this rock during trail maintenance. Gatekeeper will never be the same.

Rock ledges and drop-offs are common on the Rubicon. Travis chooses a good line to come down with his XJ on 31s.

This is a view coming down into The Slabs. It's amazing how much granite there is. In fact, I think there is more rock on this trail than dirt.

3 and 4.5 inches of lift, at least one locker, and they were on 31s. This would be the first Rubicon experience for Dustin, Tom, and John.

We all made sure we were prepared for the trip, and that also included having trail toilets. Sanitation problems became so bad in 2004 that a popular area near the trail (Spider Lake) was closed. We wanted to make sure that we weren't part of the problem and were prepared to pack out everything we brought in!

Tom really had his XJ loaded to the hilt, and we think that's what caused his rear main seal to puke oil going up the hill towards Lake Tahoe. We stopped for pizza and decided what to do about Tom's rear main seal. After pizza, we stopped by the local Kragens Auto Parts, which stayed open to help us even though it was 5 minutes after closing time. We picked up a new seal and oil pan gasket and decided to head for Loon Lake. Luckily, the rear main quit leaking, but we were prepared just in case. We pulled into Loon Lake about 7:30 pm and found a camping spot next to a group from Washington with two nicely built XJs. We enjoyed the evening around the campfire in anticipation of what the Rubicon would bring.

The following morning, we packed up and prepared to hit the trail. The weather was perfect, and, other than the fact that the mosquitoes were out in full force, we couldn't have been more pleased.

The group makes its way along the trail. Staying on the trail and keeping it clean will help keep it open for others to enjoy in the future.

Jeep XJ Profile: The Reno 4x4 XJs Do the Rubicon CONTINUED

On our hike to go see the waterfalls, we stop to take in the beautiful scenery of Buck Island Lake. Part of the fun of owning a Jeep is all the great places it can take you.

Dustin getting it on a big rock. Smooth granite with a fine coating of dust can be very slick, which adds to the challenge.

The first obstacle going in from Loon is the infamous Gatekeeper. Dustin and I had no problems on 35s, but we knew it would be a challenge for the guys on 31s! Tom got high-centered and ended up taking a strap. Travis blasted right through it, which didn't surprise us really, because we were used to his driving style: Point the Jeep in the right direction and GO! Everyone nearby better make clear! We think that may have been the wrong thing for John to see, because he decided that he wasn't ready to do it. John was wise, and he made the right decision. In my opinion, you either need to be crazy or have nerves of steel to try to do the 'Con in an XJ on 31s! John's Jeep had the smallest number of modifications and he had the least amount of driving experience between us all, so we don't fault him one bit for wanting to turn back. He'll be ready next year!

We took some time to enjoy the slabs, had lunch, and continued up the trail. As expected, the trail was very wet for that time of year. It seemed like every 100 yards there was another water hole on the trail, and we didn't have any idea how deep they were. Having a snorkel, I didn't mind, but the guys on 31s were a little concerned.

At Little Sluice we split up; Tom and Travis took the bypass up and around to the left and Dustin and I went up the rock face to the right. We met up with Jefe there, driving a built CJ8 Scrambler, who joined us on our way down to Buck Island Lake.

The next day we did a little wheeling. We took a hike to see the waterfalls, did some fishing, and enjoyed ourselves around camp. It was a beautiful day.

The following day, we broke camp and headed toward the Springs. Dustin took a bad turn and got a very big dent

Dustin at the top of Big Sluice, which is a 1/8-mile or so section of trail that is infamous for rear quarter panel dents and broken taillights on XJs.

This is the top of Cadillac Hill where everyone stops to take their group pictures. No wonder; the views are magnificent.

in one of his rear doors. Going through Big Sluice, I got high-centered on a big rock but didn't pick up any body damage as I did the year before (hooray!). We eventually made it down to the Springs to eat lunch.

After lunch, I wanted to test the snorkel and ended up getting the Jeep stuck in 4 feet of water (the details of that little adventure can be found in Chapter 7). Dustin winched me out and I tried to drain as much water out of the interior as I could. The snorkel worked great, but I knew the cleanup after this trip was going to suck.

We enjoyed going up Cadillac Hill, but at the top, we had a few trail fixes that needed to be made. Travis had a U-joint in his front axle that was about to go, so he replaced the shaft with a spare. Dustin had blown a tie-rod end, so he ended up replacing the tie-rod. And I was still scooping water out of the interior with a paper cup!

After that, it was a relatively easy ride out to Tahoe, but there was a lot of water on the trail, and a few of those water holes were very deep. We passed a small SUV that had engine trouble. A guy in a Wrangler was pulling him out (Jeepers sure are nice guys, aren't we?) and he told us the guy "got stuck in one of them puddles." That guy might be buying a Jeep as his next vehicle . . . if he's smart!

We had fun at the staging area testing our horns. None of them worked any more because of all the water we went through, but they did make some pretty interesting sounds! It was a great trip and we made it through without any major damage. Going through the Rubicon is something you never forget. We're already anticipating the next chance we get to do the 'Con! ■

STOCK CHEROKEE SPECS

Author's note: In 2003, several Cherokee owners (including myself) decided to create a list of stock specs that could be a useful resource for those seeking information. This list was originally created and listed on JeepForum.com, but has since been copied many times and appears on many different Jeep-related websites, usually as bits and pieces of the list, or old versions that had since been updated. I am including it as part of this book because it is such a good resource, but I cannot take full credit. It was a huge effort to put this together, and that credit should go to those members of JeepForum who helped me with this project. The list has been edited slightly for use in this book.

Common Design

All XJs were built as a unibody design with the body and frame rails tied together as one, as opposed to a body-on-frame design. All XJs have front and rear solid axles. The suspension consists of coil springs for the front and leaf springs for the rear. All XJs came with disc brakes in the front and drums in the rear.

Dimensions

Small differences may occur depending on optional equipment or trim level.

Wheelbase = 101.4 inches
Overall length = 165.3 to 168.8 inches
Overall width = 67.9 to 70.5 inches
Track = 58 inches
Height = 64 inches
Height with roof rack = 66.8 inches
Ground clearance (from differentials) = 7.3 to 8.3 inches
Approach angle = 37.6 to 38 degrees
Departure angle = 31 to 32.1 degrees
Breakover angle = 21 to 21.9 degrees
Curb weight 2wd = 2,891 to 2,993 pounds
Curb weight 4wd = 3,057 to 3,386 pounds
Cargo capacity = 71.0 cubic feet

Body

The body comes in both two-door and four-door styles with a rear hatch (lift gate). In 1994, side-impact beams were added in the doors and the roof was strengthened. The third brake light was added to the top of the liftgate. In 1996, the body structure was strengthened again, although it was not noticeable in appearance.

In 1997, the body and interior was redesigned to freshen it up a bit. Most noticeably, the body got smoother lines by changing the bumpers, flares, and moldings. The front fender was trimmed just below the headlights and replaced with plastic bumper end caps that wrap around to the wheelwell. The liftgate was also changed from fiberglass to sheet metal. The windshield washer bottle was moved to the inside of the driver-side front fender.

Engines

2.5L carbureted I4: 105 hp @ 5,000 rpm, 132 ft-lbs @ 2,800 rpm; used in 1984–1985 models

2.5L TBI (fuel injected) I4: 117 hp @ 5,000 rpm, 135 ft-lbs @ 3,500 rpm; used in 1986 and updated in 1987–1990 to 121 hp

2.5L MPI (multi-port injection) I4: 130 hp @ 5,250 rpm, 139 ft-lbs @ 3,250 rpm; used in 1991–2000

GM 2.8L V-6: 115 hp @ 4,800 rpm, 145 ft-lbs @ 2,400 rpm; used in 1984–1986

Renault 2.1L 4-cyl Turbo Diesel: 85 hp @ 3,750 rpm, 132 ft-lbs @ 2,750 rpm; used in 1985–1987

Italian VM 2.5L Turbo Diesel: 140 hp, 236 ft-lbs; used in overseas XJs

4.0L I6 EFI Power Tech: 177 hp @ 4,750 rpm, 220 ft-lbs @ 4,000 rpm; used in 1987–1990

4.0L I6 MPI Power Tech H.O.: 190 hp @ 4,750 rpm, 220 ft-lbs @ 4,000 rpm; used in 1991–1995 and updated in 1996–2001 to 225 ft-lbs @ 3,000 rpm; 2000–2001 models use a distributorless ignition system

Transmissions

Manual Transmissions

AX4 4-speed: manufactured by Aisin; used 1984–1986 with 2.5L I4 and 2.8L V-6 engines

T4 & T5, 4- and 5-speeds: manufactured by BorgWarner; used 1984–1986 with 2.5L I4 and 2.8L V-6 engines

BA10/5 5-speed manual: manufactured by Peugeot; used up to 1989

AX5 5-speed manual: manufactured by Aisin; used with 2.8L V-6 and 1987+ with 2.5L I4

AX15 5-speed manual: manufactured by Aisin; used with 4.0L I6 engines

NV3550 5-speed manual: manufactured by New Venture; used in 2000–2001 in SE models with 4.0L I6 engines

Automatic Transmissions

Torqueflite 904 3-speed automatic: used 1984–1986 with 2.8L V-6 and 2.5L I4 engines

30RH 3-speed automatic: used with 2.5L I4 engine 1994–2000

AW4 4-speed automatic: electronically controlled, manufactured by Aisin; used 1987–2001 (1987–1991 models include a Power/Comfort button that adjusts the shift points)

Transfer Cases

The transfer cases used are all chain-driven with aluminum housings. NP stands for "New Process," which is the manufacturer. The newer ones are NV, which stands for "New Venture." It is the same transfer case with a different name.

NP207 Command-Trac: part-time only, 2.61:1 ratio low range; used 1984–1987

Transmission Gear Ratios

Manual Transmissions

Transmission	1st	2nd	3rd	4th	5th	Rev
T4	4.02:1	2.37:1	1.50:1	1.00:1	N/A	–
T5	4.02:1	2.37:1	1.50:1	1.00:1	0.76:1	–
BA10/5	3.99:1	2.33:1	1.44:1	1.00:1	0.79:1	–
AX5	3.93:1	2.33:1	1.45:1	1.00:1	0.85:1	4.72:1
AX15	3.83:1	2.33:1	1.44:1	1.00:1	0.79:1	4.22:1
NV3550	4.01:1	2.32:1	1.40:1	1.00:1	0.78:1	3.55:1

Automatic Transmissions

Transmission	1st	2nd	3rd	4th	Rev
TF904	2.45:1	1.45:1	1.00:1	N/A	–
30RH	2.74:1	1.54:1	1.00:1	N/A	–
AW4	2.804:1	1.531:1	1.00:1	0.753:1	2.393:1

Special thanks to these guys who supplied information for this page: brcomputer, TroyBoyM, glenzx, ageofzeppelin, balloo93, MJR, zappa UK, Amethyst, joeldavid, cbremer, 91XJLimited, SV1CEC, Jeep#4, White-Knight, Scs748, and BBJeepXJ89.

NP231 Command-Trac: part-time only, 2.72:1 ratio low range, shift pattern 2H - 4H - N - 4L; used 1987–2001

NP228/NP229 Selec-Trac: 4Hi (full-time) - N - 4Lo (part-time); used 1984–1987

NP242 Selec-Trac: part-time OR full-time, 2.72:1 ratio low range, shift pattern 2WD - 4part-time - 4full-time - N - 4LO; used 1987–2001

Driveshafts

Front Driveshaft

For 1984–1987 XJs (NP207), the front shaft is a GKN-style shaft. On 1987–2001 XJs (NP231/242) the front is a double-cardan two-piece driveshaft with a CV joint at the transfer case end.

Rear Driveshaft

The rear is a one-piece shaft with standard U-joints at both ends. The slip yoke is located on the output shaft of the transfer case. On 1984–1995 models, the yoke slides in and out of the transfer case and is lubricated internally by the ATF. On 1996–2001 XJs, due to a design change, the slip yoke is external (does not slide in and out of the transfer case). This slip yoke is covered with a rubber boot.

Axles

Front Axles

Dana 30 high pinion: reverse cut, 27-spline, 1.16-inch-diameter shafts, 7.13-inch ring gear; used 1984–1999 (some axles through 1991 are vacuum disconnect, 1992-on are non-disconnect, 1989–1995 with ABS have 5-297x U-joints, all 1995-on have 5-297x U-joints, all others have 5-260x U-joints)

Dana 30 low pinion: standard cut, 27-spline, 1.16-inch-diameter shafts, 7.13-inch ring gear, 5-297x U-joints; used 2000–2001

Rear Axles

Note: Dana 35 axles are sometimes referred to as Dana 35C. The "C" does not stand for C-clip. It stands for "custom," meaning it came from Dana unfinished.

Note on Chrysler 8.25-inch axles: None of these axles were used on XJs with ABS brakes. If you have ABS, you have the Dana 35. Without ABS, you could have either axle. The 8.25-inch axles use C-clips.

Dana 35 non-C-clip: 27-spline, 1.18-inch-diameter shafts, 7.58-inch ring gear, 2.62-inch axle tube; used 1984–1989

Dana 35 C-clip: 27-spline, 1.18-inch-diameter shafts, 7.58-inch ring gear, 2.62-inch axle tube; used 1990–2001

Chrysler 8.25: 27-spline, 1.17-inch-diameter shafts, 8.25-inch ring gear, 3-inch axle tube; used 1991–1996

Chrysler 8.25: 29-spline, 1.21-inch-diameter shafts, 8.25-inch ring gear, 3-inch axle tube; used 1997–2001

Dana 44 non–C-clip: 30-spline, 1.31-inch-diameter shafts, 8.5-inch ring gear, 2.75-inch axle tube; used 1987–1989 on some (not all) XJs equipped with towing package.

Gearing

3.07:1 used with 4.0L engine and manual transmission

3.31:1 only available on older (pre-1987) two-door XJs with "Fuel Economy" package

3.55:1 used with 4.0L engine and automatic transmission

3.73:1 found in some XJs with the towing package

4.10:1 used with 2.5L engine usually, and older XJs with the "Off-Highway Vehicle" package

4.56:1 rare but can be found on some older models with 2.5L engine and automatic transmission

Cooling Systems

Open style: any normal cooling system used today. Opposite of closed style described below.

Closed style: has no radiator cap and utilizes a pressure bottle. This style cooling system was used in 1987–1990 XJs.

Airbags

Driver-side airbag (mechanical) was added in 1995. Passenger-side airbag was added in 1997. Airbags also changed from mechanical to electronic in 1997.

Production Numbers

Number of XJs built per year:

1984: 93,326	1994: 123,391
1985: 120,328	1995: 120,234
1986: 107,225	1996: 286,463
1987: 139,295	1997: 258,958
1988: 187,136	1998: 182,845
1989: 207,216	1999: 186,116
1990: 151,230	2000: 165,590
1991: 151,578	(Freedom
1992: 137,826	Edition: 2,821)
1993: 144,961	2001: 120,454

Total number of XJs built from 1984 through 2001: 2,884,172.

Trim Levels

1984: Base, Wagoneer, Pioneer, Chief

1985: Base, Wagoneer, Pioneer, Chief, Laredo

1986: Base, Wagoneer, Pioneer, Chief, Laredo

1987: Base, Wagoneer, Pioneer, Chief, Laredo, Limited

1988: Base, Wagoneer, Pioneer, Chief, Laredo, Limited, Sport

1989: Base, Wagoneer, Pioneer, Chief, Laredo, Limited, Sport

1990: Base, Wagoneer, Pioneer, Chief, Laredo, Limited, Sport

1991: Base, Briarwood, Chief, Laredo, Limited, Sport

1992: Base, Briarwood, Chief, Laredo, Limited, Sport

1993: Base, Sport, Country

1994: SE, Sport, Country

1995: SE, Sport, Country

1996: SE, Sport, Country, Classic

1997: SE, Sport, Country

1998: SE, Sport, Classic, Limited

1999: SE, Sport, Classic, Limited

2000: SE, Sport, Classic, Limited, Freedom

2001: Sport, Limited, 60th Anniversary Edition

Other Resources

Factory Service Manuals at techauthority.daimlerchrysler.com or by calling 1-800-890-4038 (U.S.) or 1-800-387-1143 (Canada).

DaimlerChrysler E-Fiche Service Parts Catalog 1981–1996

DaimlerChrysler E-Fiche Service Parts Catalog 1997–1999

DaimlerChrysler E-Fiche Service Parts Catalog 2000

GLOSSARY

I have tried to avoid using too many abbreviations in this book, for your sake, but they are used frequently on the Internet in Jeep-related message boards, forums, and chat rooms. The following is a list of common abbreviations used, some are proper abbreviations and others you might find unconventional.

8.25: refers to the Chrysler rear axle that has an 8.25-inch ring gear

8.8: refers to the Ford rear axle that has an 8.8-inch ring gear

AA: Advance Adapters, parts manufacturer

AAL: add-a-leaf; a single leaf added to the factory leaf pack to achieve lift

ABS: Anti-lock Brake System

AEV: American Expedition Vehicles, off-road accessory manufacturer

AMC: American Motors Corporation (owned the Jeep brand until 1987)

ARB: ARB USA, off-road accessory manufacturer. Also may refer to the ARB locker made by the same company. ARB stands for Anthony Ronald Brown, the company's founder.

Articulation: see "flex"

AT: "all terrain," referring to a type of tire tread

ATF: automatic transmission fluid

BA10/5: the Peugeot manual transmission

BB: budget boost. Usually only increases 1 to 2 inches of lift.

BFG: BFGoodrich

BFH: big "F-ing" hammer

BPE: bar pin eliminators

BS: backspacing. The distance from the inner mounting surface of the wheel to the inboard edge of the rim.

Bumpsteer: when uneven road or a bump causes the wheels to steer in an unwanted direction

C4x4: Custom 4x4 Fabrications, off-road accessory manufacturer

Camber: refers to inward or outward tilt of the wheel relative to the center of the vehicle

Cat: refers to a catalytic converter that is located before the muffler on an exhaust system

Cat-back exhaust: aftermarket exhaust replacing everything after the catalytic converter

Caster: refers to forward or rearward tilt of the steering knuckle from vertical

CB: citizens band radio

CCV: crank case ventilation

CJ: the classic short-wheelbased Jeep from 1945 with different versions made into the 1980s

Closed cooling system: This is the cooling system found in older models that has to be "burped" when fluid is added, or "hot spots" occur in the cooling system as air is trapped in the passages

COG: center of gravity

Command-Trac: part-time 4WD system (NP231 transfer case)

CPS: crank position sensor

CV joint: constant velocity joint

D30: refers to the Dana 30 front axle

D35: refers to the Dana 35 rear axle

D44: refers to the Dana 44 front or rear axle

DD: daily driver

Differential: short for differential. The center section on the axle that contain the gears, sometimes called the "pumpkin."

DOT: Department of Transportation

DPA: drop pitman arm

Drag link: the bar connecting the pitman arm and the passenger-side steering knuckle (driver-side knuckle on RHD Jeeps)

DS: driveshaft

DW: death wobble, violent shaking of front end due to a worn or loose part, or bad alignment

EFI: electronic fuel injection

FSM: factory service manual

Flex: suspension travel usually when one wheel is drooping down and the other wheel on the axle is "stuffed," or pushed up into the wheelwell. Also referred to as articulation.

GPS: Global Positioning System

Hack-N-Tap: Rubicon Express cut-and-tap SYE kit

Header: refers to exhaust header. Used to channel exhaust to exhaust pipe.

HD: heavy-duty

HO: "High Output" referring to the upgraded 4.0L inline 6-cylinder engine

---

HP: horsepower

HP: high-pinion, as in HP30 (high-pinion Dana 30) or HP44 (high-pinion Dana 44)

I4: inline 4-cylinder engine

I6: inline 6-cylinder engine

IFS: independent front suspension

JF: JeepForum.com

KJ: Jeep Liberty (also called Cherokee overseas but this is NOT the same vehicle as the XJ)

LCA: lower control arm

LHD: left-hand drive (steering wheel is on the left)

Locker: traction device that locks both axle shafts together

LP: low-pinion, as in LP30 (low-pinion Dana 30) or LP44 (low-pinion Dana 44)

LSD: limited-slip differential, sometimes referred to as "posi-traction"

MAP: manifold absolute pressure sensor

MJ: Jeep Comanche pickup (1986–1992)

M.O.R.E.: Mountain Off-Road Enterprises, off-road accessory manufacturer

MPI: multi-port (or multipoint) fuel injection

MT: mud terrain, referring to a type of tire tread

MT/R: Maximum Traction Reinforced, a tire made by Goodyear

NAXJA: North American XJ Association (NAXJA.org)

NSS: neutral safety switch

O2: oxygen sensor

OBA: onboard air

OBDI: first generation onboard diagnostics engine control computer

OBDII: second generation onboard diagnostics found in 1996–2000 vehicles. Includes a port under the driver-side dash for scanner plug in.

OEM: original equipment manufacturer

Off-camber: a slope of the terrain causing the vehicle to lean far to one side

OME: Old Man Emu, off-road accessory manufacturer

Open cooling system: the cooling system used on new models

Open differentials: They do not have a traction device such as a locker or limited slip

Open element filter: A cone or cylinder shaped air filter that is not shielded under the hood. These are used in place of the factory air box.

ORO: OffRoadOnly, off-road accessory manufacturer

OTK: refers to "over-the-knuckle," a type of steering setup

Pitman arm: the arm that attaches the drag link to the steering box

PSI: pounds per square inch

RE: Rubicon Express, off-road accessory manufacturer

RHD: right-hand drive (steering wheel is on the right)

RRO: Rocky Road Outfitters, off-road accessory manufacturer

RTV: stands for "room temperature vulcanization." Also known as gasket maker.

Selec-Trac: 4WD system that includes both full-time and part-time modes (NP242 transfer case)

Siping: small cuts added to the lugs of a tire to improve traction on wet or icy surfaces

Steering stabilizer: the small shock attached to the drag link that absorbs minor vibration in the steering

Sway bar: also known as "anti-sway bar" or "stabilizer bar," it reduces body roll during turns

Sway bar disconnects: the linkage that allows the sway bar to be disconnected for off-road use, allowing for more articulation of the suspension. Also called "quick disconnects."

SWB: short wheelbase, like the CJ or Wrangler

SYE: slip yoke eliminator. A kit that converts the slip yoke to a fixed yoke on the transfer case output shaft.

T-case: transfer case

TB: throttle body

TCU: transmission control unit

TPS: throttle position sensor

Tie-rod: the bar that connects the driver-side steering knuckle and the drag link. On RHD Jeeps, it attaches to the passenger-side steering knuckle.

TJ: Jeep Wrangler (1997–2006)

Trac-Lok: the factory option limited-slip differential

Track bar: the bar that keeps the front axle centered under the body

TRE: tie-rod end

U-joint: universal joint

UCA: upper control arm

VIN: vehicle identification number

WJ: Jeep Grand Cherokee (1999–2004)

WK: Jeep Grand Cherokee (2005–present)

WMS-WMS: wheel-mounting surface to wheel-mounting surface, or the width of an axle

XJ: Jeep Cherokee (1984–2001)

YJ: Jeep Wrangler (1987–1995)

ZJ: Jeep Grand Cherokee (1993–1998)

SOURCE GUIDE

Advance Adapters
4320 Aerotech Center Way
Paso Robles, CA 93446
800-350-2223
advanceadapters.com

AJ's Offroad Armor
ajsoffroadarmor.com

American Expedition Vehicles
P.O. Box 621
Missoula, MT 59806
406-251-2100
aev-conversions.com

ARB 4x4 Accessories
720 S.W. 34th Street
Renton, WA 98055-4814
425-264-1391
arbusa.com

Auburn Gear
400 E. Auburn Drive
Auburn, IN 46706
260-925-3200
auburngear.com

Aussie Locker
Torq-Masters Technology, Inc.
3177 Latta Road
Rochester, NY 14612
585-723-1489
Aussielocker.com

AutoHomeUSA
112 N. Curry Street
Carson City, NV 89703
888-852-2359
autohomeus.com

BDS Suspension
102 S. Michigan Avenue
Coldwater, MI 49036
517-279-8807
bds-suspension.com

Blue Ribbon Coalition
4555 Burley Drive, Suite A
Pocatello, ID 83202
208-237-1008
sharetrails.com

Blue Torch Fabworks
P.O. Box 8367
Dorthanm, AL 36304
866-725-2795
bluetorchfab.com

BushWacker
6710 N. Catlin Avenue
Portland, Oregon 97203
800-234-8920
BushWacker.com

C-ROK Engineering and Fabrication
8360 S. Stephanie Lane
Tempe, AZ 85284
480-699-2099
c-rok.com

ComancheClub.com

Custom 4x4 Fabrication
11825 S.E. 109th
Oklahoma City, OK 73165
405-799-7599
custom4x4fabrication.com

Currie Enterprises, Inc.
1480 N. Tustin Avenue
Anaheim, CA 92807
714-528-6957
currieenterprises.com

D & C Extreme
719-510-5027
Dandcextreme.com

DaimlerChrysler
P.O. Box 21-8004
Auburn Hills, MI 48321
800-992-1997
Jeep.com

Detours Manufacturing
203-315-8111
detoursusa.com

DPG Off-Road
P.O. Box 190
Rose Hill, KS 67133
316-776-9900
dpgoffroad.com

DynoMax
2701 N. Dettman Road
Jackson, MI 49201
734-384-7806
dynomax.com

Del Albright of Albright Enterprises
Mokelumne Hill, CA 95245
delalbright.com

ericsxj.com/fs.fed.us

Goferit Offroad Inc.
2511 Overbrook Drive
Greensboro, NC 27408
336-317-7130
goferitoffroad.com

Hanson Offroad
877-757-9779
Hansonoffroad.com

Haynes North America, Inc.
861 Lawrence Drive
Newbury Park, CA 91320-1514
805-498-6703

HD Offroad Engineering LLC
hdoffroadengineering.myshopify.com/

High Angle Driveline
530-877-2875
highangledriveline.com

JCR Offroad
269-372-2842
jcroffroad.com

Jeepers and Creepers
415-387-2323
JeepersandCreepers.com

Jeepforum.com

Jeepin' Outfitters
469-569-5663
Jeepinoutfitters.com
Jeepin.com

JKS Manufacturing, Inc.
P.O. Box 98
Alliance, NE 69301-0098
308-762-6949
jksmfg.com

K&N Engineering, Inc.
1455 Citrus Street
Riverside, CA 92502
800-858-3333
knfilters.com

Mepco 4x4
5241 S 300 W
Murray, UT 84107
801-266-3726
mepco4x4.com

Man-A-Fre
1775 N. Surveyor Avenue
Simi Valley, CA 93063
805-578-8712
man-a-fre.com

M.I.T. Drivetrain Specialists
1112 Pioneer Way
El Cajon, CA 92020
619-579-7727

Mountain Off-Road Enterprises
P.O. Box 843
Rifle, CO 81650
970-625-0500
mountainoffroad.com

Napier Precision Products
Napierprecisionproducts.com

New Process Gear Division
6600 New Venture Gear Drive
East Syracuse, NY 13057
315-432-4000
newventuregear.com

North American XJ Association
naxja.org

Off Road Only, LLC
651-644-2323
offroadonly.com

Olympic 4x4 Products
2645 S. Yates Avenue
City of Commerce, CA 90040
323-726-6988
4x4products.com

OR-Fab
Performance Automotive Group, Inc.
3651 N. Hwy 89
PO Box 3450
Chino Valley, AZ 86323
928-636-7080
Orfab.com

Proto Fab
P.O. Box 967
Dewey, AZ 86327
928-632-0216
protofab4x4.com

RIGID Fabrication & Manufacturing
801-450-0928
rigidco.com

rockcrawler.com

Rocky Road Outfitters
888-801-7271
rocky-road.com

Rough Country
800-222-7023
roughcountry.com

Rubicon Express
3290 Monier Circle, #100
Rancho Cordova, CA 95742
877-367-7824
rubiconexpress.com

Ruff Stuff Specialties
3237 Rippey Rd #200
Loomis, CA 95650
916-600-1945
Ruffstuffspecialties.com

Rugged Ridge
Ruggedridge.com

Rusty's Off-Road Products
7161 Steele Station Road
Rainbow City, AL 35906
256-442-0607
rustysoffroad.com

Skid Row Automotive, Inc.
505 Bentzel Road
Shermans Dale, PA 17090
skidplates.com

Skyjacker Suspensions
212 Stevenson Street
West Monroe, LA 71292
318-388-0816
skyjacker.com

Smittybilt
400 W. Artesia Blvd
Compton, CA 90220
888-717-5797
Smittybilt.com

Sway-A-Way
20724 Lassen Street
Chatsworth, CA 91311
818-700-9712
swayaway.com

T&J Performance Center
1002 W. Collins Avenue
Orange, CA 92867
714-633-0991
tandjperformance.com

T&T Customs, Inc.
1803 C S. Greeley Highway
Cheyenne, WY 82007
307-214-7754
tntcustoms.com

Tera Manufacturing, Inc.
5251 S. Commerce Drive
Murray, UT 84107-4711
801-288-2585
teraflx.com

Tom Wood's Custom Drive Shafts
877-497-4238
4xshaft.com

Tomken, Inc.
752 U.S. Hwy 24 N.
Buena Vista, CO 81211
719-395-2526
tomken.com

TrailReady by RSI
1304 80th Street S.W.
Everett, WA 98203
425-353-6776
trailready.com

United Four Wheel Drive Associations
7135 S. Royal Springs Drive
Shelbyville, IN 46176
800-448-3932
ufwda.org

Warn Industries, Inc.
12900 S.E. Capps Road
Clackamas, OR 97015
800-543-9276
warn.com

Warrior Products
16850 SW Upper Boones Ferry Rd.
Suite A
Durham, OR 97224
888-220-6861
Warriorproducts.com

Yukon Gear & Axle
636 W. Diversey Parkway #180
Chicago, IL 60614-1511
yukongear.com